ANALYSIS
WITHOUT
PARALYSIS

10 TOOLS TO MAKE BETTER
STRATEGIC DECISIONS

BABETTE E. BENSOUSSAN • CRAIG S. FLEISHER

Vice President, Publisher: Tim Moore
Associate Publisher and Director of Marketing: Amy Neidlinger
Acquisitions Editor: Martha Cooley
Editorial Assistant: Heather Luciano
Development Editor: Russ Hall
Operations Manager: Gina Kanouse
Digital Marketing Manager: Julie Phifer
Publicity Manager: Laura Czaja
Assistant Marketing Manager: Megan Colvin
Marketing Assistant: Brandon Smith
Cover Designer: Alan Clements
Managing Editor: Kristy Hart
Project Editor: Betsy Harris
Copy Editor: Language Logistics
Proofreader: Williams Woods Publishing
Senior Indexer: Cheryl Lenser
Senior Compositor: Gloria Schurick
Manufacturing Buyer: Dan Uhrig

© 2008 by Pearson Education, Inc.
Publishing as FT Press
Upper Saddle River, New Jersey 07458

FT Press offers excellent discounts on this book when ordered in quantity for bulk purchases or special sales. For more information, please contact U.S. Corporate and Government Sales, 1-800-382-3419, corpsales@pearsontechgroup.com. For sales outside the U.S., please contact International Sales at international@pearson.com.

Printed in the United States of America

First Printing June 2008

ISBN-10: 0-13-236180-9
ISBN-13: 978-0-13-236180-4

Pearson Education LTD.
Pearson Education Australia PTY, Limited.
Pearson Education Singapore, Pte. Ltd.
Pearson Education North Asia, Ltd.
Pearson Education Canada, Ltd.
Pearson Educatión de Mexico, S.A. de C.V.
Pearson Education—Japan
Pearson Education Malaysia, Pte. Ltd.

Library of Congress Cataloging-in-Publication Data.

Bensoussan, Babette E.

 Analysis without paralysis : 10 tools to make better strategic decisions / Babette E. Bensoussan, Craig Fleisher.

    p. cm.

  ISBN 0-13-236180-9 (hbk. : alk. paper) 1. Business intelligence—Evaluation. 2. Competition—Evaluation. 3. Strategic planning. 4. Business planning. I. Fleisher, Craig S. II. Title.

 HD38.7.B4555 2008

 658.4'01—dc22

                          2008007898

This book is dedicated to our families.

Babette E. Bensoussan and Craig S. Fleisher

Contents

PART I: **Introduction** 1

Chapter 1   Business Management and the Role of
                Analysis 3
                The Increasing Need for Effective Analysis. 8
                Concluding Observations 11

Chapter 2   The Analysis Process 15
                What Is Analysis?. 18

PART II: **Analysis Tools** 27

Chapter 3   BCG Growth/Share Portfolio Matrix 29
                Description and Purpose 29
                Strengths 35
                Weaknesses 36
                How to Do It 38

Chapter 4   Competitor Analysis 49
                Description and Purpose 49
                Strengths 51
                Weaknesses 51
                How to Do It 52

Chapter 5   Financial Ratio and Statement Analysis . . .67
                Description and Purpose 67
                Strengths 70
                Weaknesses 70
                How to Do It 73

Chapter 6   Five Forces Industry Analysis 95

Description and Purpose 95

Strengths 100

Weaknesses 101

How to Do It 102

Endnote 109

Chapter 7   Issue Analysis 111

Description and Purpose 111

Strengths 113

Weaknesses 114

How to Do It 115

Chapter 8   Political Risk Analysis 131

Description and Purpose 131

Strengths 132

Weaknesses 134

How to Do It 135

Endnotes 150

Chapter 9   Scenario Analysis .151

Description and Purpose 151

Strengths 156

Weaknesses 157

How to Do It 158

Endnote 167

Chapter 10 Macroenvironmental
(STEEP/PEST) Analysis 169

Description and Purpose 169

Strengths 172

Weaknesses 174

How to Do It 175

Chapter 11 SWOT Analysis 183

             Description and Purpose 183

             Strengths 188

             Weaknesses 189

             How to Do It 190

Chapter 12 Value Chain Analysis 199

             Description and Purpose 199

             Strengths 204

             Weaknesses 205

             How to Do It 206

             Index 221

Acknowledgments

To write this book I have had to stand on the shoulders of many—my coauthor Craig Fleisher who gave me so much support and understanding during my moments of crisis; my wonderful husband whose patience, nurturing, and understanding provided a safe space for me to work; my family and dear friends who understood the many times I was not always there for them while completing this book. To the many shoulders at FT Press, thank you for making this book happen. We could not have done it without you. And finally, I would like to thank my many clients and colleagues for the challenges and questioning that made me realize there had to be a simpler way to do business analysis without being left in a state of paralysis. I hope this little book provides you with the necessary tools to solve some of your problems.

—Babette Bensoussan

I would like to thank my long-time coauthor and friend Babette Bensoussan for all her hard and thoughtful work toward making this book a reality. She worked tirelessly while also balancing numerous other assignments, issues, and tasks. I also want to thank my family members, friends, and colleagues for remaining patient and understanding during the time that I was working on completing the book. FT Press has also been their usual helpful selves throughout the duration of this writing effort. I also want to thank individuals at several universities who have been working with and supportive of me, mainly including the Leicester Business School—De Montfort University (UK) and my good friend Sheila Wright, with whom I am sharing in the supervision of several doctoral students as well as numerous research projects; and Tampere University of Technology (Finland) and Mika Hannula, who directs the of the Institute of Business Information Management and Logistics, where I am appointed as a docent and also participate in the annual eBRF conferences. Last, but not least, I want to express my appreciation to the various bodies that provided funding and other forms of support to me along the way in developing this book, especially the University of Windsor through its Windsor Research Leadership Chair and Odette Research Chairs and Dean Allan Conway in the Odette School of Business, who has been generous in allowing me to pursue the completion of this book.

—**Craig S. Fleisher**

About the Authors

Babette E. Bensoussan is Managing Director of The Mind-Shifts Group, a company specializing in competitive intelligence, strategic planning, and strategic marketing projects in the Australasia region. Babette is widely recognized and sought after for her international expertise in competitive analysis and has provided mentoring and training to executives and organizations to assist with the delivery and implementation of competitive intelligence. She has undertaken major studies for and consulted to Australian and global Fortune 500 companies and has undertaken over 300 projects in a wide range of industries and markets.

In 2006 she was recognized for her work in this field by being presented with the highest and most prestigious award in the field of competitive intelligence—the SCIP Meritorious Award.

Apart from her active business responsibilities, Babette has taught competitive intelligence at both the Sydney Graduate School of Management, University of Western Sydney, and at Bond University in the undergraduate business and MBA programs. She has published numerous articles on strategic planning, competitive intelligence, and strategic marketing and is an invited speaker and guest lecturer both domestically and internationally.

Babette has shared her knowledge of competitive business analysis by coauthoring two books. *Strategic and Competitive Analysis* and *Business and Competitive Analysis* have both been the top-selling books in this field since being published in 2003 and 2007 respectively.

Craig S. Fleisher holds the Windsor Research Leadership Chair and is Professor of Management, Odette School of Business, University of Windsor, Canada. Recognized as one of Canada's top MBA professors by *Canadian Business*, he has previously served as dean, MBA director, and/or endowed research chair at several Canadian universities, is a Docent of the Institute of Business Information Management and Logistics at Tampere University of Technology in

Finland, and held or holds adjunct positions at universities in Australia, New Zealand, South Africa, and the United Kingdon. His Ph.D. is from the Katz Graduate School of Business, University of Pittsburgh. A contributing member of various association, corporate, and journal editorial boards, he is a past President and Fellow of the international Society of Competitive Intelligence Professionals, founder and inaugural chair of the Board of Trustees of the Competitive Intelligence Foundation (Washington, DC), founding editor of the *Journal of Competitive Intelligence and Management*, and founding member of the International Association of Business and Society. Recognized as the 2007 Advisor of the Year in Canada by the Golden Key International Honour Society, Craig has authored or edited nine books (several also have multiple foreign language translations) and scores of articles and chapters in the area of applied strategy, competitive intelligence and analysis, or performance management. His most recent book was *Business and Competitive Analysis* (FT Press, 2007). A well-traveled speaker, he regularly advises leading corporations, associations, and public sector agencies on competitive intelligence and analysis.

Part
I

Introduction

Chapter 1 Business Management and the Role of Analysis   3

Chapter 2 The Analysis Process   15

1

Business Management and the Role of Analysis

In today's information age, businessmen and businesswomen must increasingly be able to make sense of their competition, environments, organizations, and strategies to be successful. Business management is a way of conducting an organization that has as an ultimate objective the development of values, managerial capabilities, organizational responsibilities, and administrative systems that link strategic, tactical, and operational decision making at all hierarchical levels and across all lines of authority.

One of the key tasks of today's business executives is to participate in and contribute to their organizations' strategies. Sadly, strategy is an overused word that means different things to different people. Even distinguished management scholars and senior executives can be hard pressed to define it or to agree on what it entails.

Although we really do not want to muddy the waters and add further to the lengthy list of definitions out there, we do know with confidence that winning strategies are based on originality and uniqueness—being "different" than competitors in ways that customers value. The idea of these differences has been defined by economists to mean competencies, and in strategic management terms, this means trying to develop distinctive organizational resources and competencies. These competencies should then be leveraged through clearly thought-out strategies into a competitive advantage in light of the organization's market.

A competitive advantage is the distinct way an organization is positioned in the market to obtain an edge over its competitors. This status is most commonly evidenced by the organization's ability to generate and maintain sustained levels of profitability above the industry average. The process that is primarily associated with helping an organization to attain competitive advantage is strategic planning, which can be defined as a disciplined and systematic effort to fulfill specifications of an organization's strategy as well as the assignment of responsibilities for its execution. This process is shown as follows in Figure 1.1.

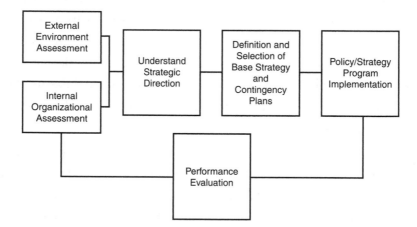

Figure 1.1   A generic strategic planning process

Management decisions in the strategy development process are concerned with the following:

- **The scope of the organization's activities.** Where are we going to operate? What customers will we target? Which competitors will we avoid? What parts of the value chain will we emphasize? What will we do ourselves and what will we outsource?

- **The matching of an organization's activities to its environment.** This is the idea of finding a strategy that creates a desirable level of "fit."

- **The matching of an organization's activities to its resource capability.** This requires working within our means while winning customers and generating profits.

- **The implications for change throughout the organization.** These are likely to be complex in nature and will require excellence in execution or strategy implementation.

- **The allocation and reallocation of significant resources of an organization.** This requires us to seek resource optimization in using our assets where they can be maximized.

- **The values, expectations, and goals of those influencing strategy.** This means that decision makers understand what is happening and have a clear sense of where the organization needs to go both now and into the future.

- **The direction the organization will move in the long run.** This can be over five to ten years or more, depending on the nature of change and competition affecting an industry.

Within this process, management decisions may differ depending on the timing and the responsibility of the decision makers. These decisions would most commonly be identified as strategic, tactical, or operational. By this we mean

- **Strategic decisions** have significant resource allocation impact, set precedents or tone for decisions further down the organization, are infrequent in nature and may actually be irreversible, and have a potentially material effect on the organization's competitiveness within its marketplace. They are made by top managers and affect the business direction of an organization.

- **Tactical decisions** are less all-encompassing than strategic ones and involve formulating and implementing policies for the organization. They are usually made by mid-level managers and often materially affect functions such as marketing, accounting, production, or a business unit or product as opposed to the entire organization. Tactical decisions generally have lesser resource implications than strategic decisions.

- **Operational decisions** support the day-to-day decisions needed to operate the organization and take effect over a few days or weeks. Typically made by a lower-level manager, operational decisions are distinct from tactical and strategic decisions in that they are made frequently and often "on the fly." Operational decisions tend to be highly structured, often with well-defined procedure manuals or within readily understood parameters.

Finding the means for achieving this "fit" or congruence between an organization and its (business or competitive) environment is a critical task of any senior executive and requires sound analytical efforts and some thinking about the global environment in which the organization competes.

No senior executive can be expected to know the entire competitive terrain well enough to correctly call all the shots. Within today's complex, chaotic, globally competitive environment, the pressing need for making sense, strategic thinking, and improved understanding of the competitive terrain is why organizations need to develop and enhance their analytical abilities.

Analysis needs to be done well to help organizations succeed.

But isn't analysis something that everyone learns during schooling or on the job? Can't we just get by like everybody else and rely solely on our intuition, gut, experience, and so on to succeed well into the future?

The answer to these questions is, "No"—and particularly not these days. See Table 1.1 for a brief explaination of what we do and do not mean by analysis.

At a minimum, good analysis of your competition, environment, organization, and strategy should help you deliver the following:

- Early warning of potentially developing opportunities or emerging threats in your competitive environment.
- An objective and arm's-length assessment of your organization's relative competitive position.
- The ability to help your organization to more quickly and easily adapt to changes in the environment.

TABLE 1.1   Identifying Analysis

	What Analysis *Is*	What Analysis Is *Not*
Methods	The practiced application of proven technologies.	Constant usage of industry conventions and one-off solutions.
Process	A method and set of steps designed to effectively break a situation into its component elements and recompose it in a way that addresses a challenge or question.	"We just kind of know what it is, how to do it, and fortunately, have managed to get by so far." "We hire consultants to do it for us."
Output	Actionable insight, intelligence/meaning, and implications derived from data and information.	Repackaged, reorganized, reclassified data and information. Often a summary of the information at hand. No meaningful conversion.
Data sources	Legal and ethical gathering of relevant data or information driven by the needs defined in the structuring of the analytical question.	Seeking and using data or information from illegal sources or by unethical means—often incomplete.
Support systems	Using application-relevant communication, information, and management systems to supplement your thinking.	A software application or solution you can acquire and apply "off the shelf." Magic-bullet solutions.
Timing	Provided in advance of any decisions.	Rushed to provide support to an answer that has been decided.
Communication channel	Conducted in whatever means the decision maker can best accept and use it.	Done via "formal" reports with a specific format. Always in writing.
Questions answered	What? So What? Now What?	Just something nice to know—providing no insights.
Catalyst	Yours or your boss' discussed need to know something. The need to better position your organization in its competitive marketplace.	What you think or hope is important to the executive. The need to demonstrate we are actually doing something.

- The means for basing your organization's strategic, marketing, sales, or product plans on relevant and timely insights.
- Confidence that decisions are based on systematically derived understanding that reduces ambiguity and complexity to low levels.

The driving purpose of performing analysis is to better understand your industry, context, and competitors in order to make better decisions. Improving the quality of decision making should hopefully improve the quality of strategies that provide a competitive advantage, which in turn delivers performance results that are superior to your competitors'.

The output of any analysis should be actionable—that is, future-oriented—and should help decision makers to develop better competitive strategies and tactics. Analysis results should also facilitate a better understanding than competitors have of the competitive environment and identify current and future competitors, specifically their plans and strategies. *The ultimate aim of analysis is to produce better business results!*

The Increasing Need for Effective Analysis

As indicated earlier, getting business results from analysis has become a more important facet of competitiveness in recent years due to a number of important reasons.

First, globalization has increased the absolute level of competition present in most marketplaces. In the past, a competitor could sustain marketplace advantages by being in the right place at the right time. Geographic, physical, and sociopolitical barriers kept competitors at bay and out of many marketplaces. Most of these barriers are falling or have fallen in light of vast progress made in communication, information systems, trade policy, and transportation. New competitors quickly appear when and where these marketplace barriers fade.

And new competitors may compete very differently than existing competitors. They may have learned their business in different contexts, often faced differing customer demands, utilized unique resources, and understood competition based on these unique contexts and experiences. No longer can organizations expect competitors to compete by age old "rules of the game" or "same old" industry means of competing. Sometimes, the form of competition may not even appear logical, insightful, or ethical, yet all the while being legal. Because of this new global competition, the need to thoroughly understand competitors and business contexts grows in importance.

Second, the global economy is increasingly being characterized as a *knowledge economy*. A paradigm shift, whereby a large proportion of individuals have changed their way of seeing the world and now see it from a new shared perspective, has occurred as we move further away from the industrial economy paradigm that dominated most of the last two centuries. As opposed to producing tangible "things" with plants, property, and equipment, services and related "intangibles" associated with people and what they know now constitute the largest part of GDP in most of the leading economies, and services are more knowledge-based than material-based.

Many companies are amassing data and information while at the same time not recognizing that *knowledge* is not the same thing as *information*. Because of improvements in communication channels, information is available in quantities previously unseen. Information has become increasingly infused with noise, redundancy, ambiguity, and is of lower value. It is a product in what economists call a "state of oversupply" in most developed economies, and this is also becoming true in lesser developed economies. Sustaining a competitive advantage requires companies to uniquely apply data and information, to create order out of chaos and complexity, and to leverage and transfer knowledge while striving toward acquiring expertise.

Knowledge is the capacity to act. The conversion of knowledge to business insights and action requires competence in analysis or sense making. Competence embraces such things as experience, factual understanding about industry and organizational conditions, decision-making and managerial skills, and making insightful value judgments. Competence is developed through making mistakes, practice, reflection, repetition, and training. More than ever before, the knowledge economy means that organizations will need to develop further their resources, abilities, competence, and ultimately expertise if they intend to gain or sustain a competitive advantage.

Third, the new economy is characterized by increasing imitability, whereby competitors have a greater ability than ever before to quickly replicate and copy most facets of a new product or service offering. Fending off imitators is increasingly difficult because of market complexity and the subsequent need to involve other organizations in alliances, collaborations with competitors, spin-offs, and ever-changing outsourcing and staffing arrangements between organizations. As a result of the protection of a product/service through legally recognized vehicles such as copyrights, patents, and/or trademarks, it is now easy for a competitor to manufacture around a new offering because so much information about its inner workings is available publicly. Finding this information has also gotten easier in an age where governments and international agencies must share this information with one another to establish the legal viability of a new offering. More than a few companies succeed by being "quick seconds" or "fast followers" into the marketplace and stressing their competitive abilities at getting an improved product/service offering that customers appreciate quickly after the originator.

Fourth, there are the problems and opportunities caused by increasing complexity and speed. Underlying the changing marketplace is communication and information technology that allows for the transfer of data to take place at faster rates than ever before. This change in mechanical means occurs all the while the human ability to process data remains essentially stable.

A decade or two ago a company could establish a formidable lead for several years by offering new product/service introductions. Today a company's time at the top in a market-leading position has shrunk to a *much* shorter duration; in other words, the interval a company enjoys as "market leader" has fallen to previously unforeseen levels. The cycle time underlying new product/service introductions is also shorter, and companies have to continue shrinking it while at the same time increasing the number of introductions they make to stay ahead of competitors.

Concluding Observations

As we stated earlier, all of these factors necessitate good competitive insights. And good competitive insights require effective analysis. Successful business analysis requires understanding environments, industries, and organizations. This comes from, among other things, experience, solid data and information, and the proper choice and utilization of analytical techniques.

Today's businesspeople need to do a better job of making sure that the analysis they perform is based on sound, proven methodologies. Hopefully in the future you will master a core set of methodologies that will make the way you evaluate data and information more effective and more decision-relevant. At a minimum, after reading this book, you will know at least ten methodologies to help you on your path.

This book contains ten of the more well-known and more heavily utilized analytical techniques for assessing the external and internal organizational environments (refer to Figure 1.1) and is designed to assist any businessperson who needs to develop insights and make sense of the business environment. It is based on our many decades of experience consulting, practicing, and researching how business and competitive analysis is used in all types of enterprises, whether public or private or large, medium, or small.

Our underlying premise throughout this book is that businesspeople working in any environment must have a robust and healthy selection of tools and techniques to help them answer important questions about their enterprises' abilities to compete, not only in the present, but also the future.

Uniquely, this book focuses specifically on analysis. It is not designed to be another business management or strategic planning text; on the other hand, we must admit that the processes and techniques described herein can certainly benefit strategic planners and managers. There are plenty of good titles on these topics available in most bookstores, and we routinely refer to many of them ourselves. What surprises us, though, about competitive and strategic analysis is the limited number of tools and techniques used by most businesspeople and how little genuine insight results from them when they have *scores* of techniques at their disposal!

These adverse results occur not only because some tools are badly chosen, outdated, or incorrectly used but also because they are misunderstood and/or misapplied. Even those individuals who get a good business school education may not have had the appropriate contexts, instruction, experiences, or guidance in employing these techniques effectively to deal with "real-world" sense-making challenges.

This book provides instruction on a range of tools and techniques, evaluation of each technique's strengths and weaknesses, as well as an outline of the process used to actually employ the technique. It also includes sample applications, resulting overall in that vital ingredient—insight.

Being a businessperson in an enterprise facing a high degree of competitive rivalry is difficult, especially if an individual is inexperienced and/or lacks appreciation of the art of analysis. And the analytical challenge for businesspeople today is more daunting than ever for a number of reasons, including the following:

- **Pressure for a quick judgment.** Competitors are moving fast, investors and shareholders want the quarterly performance targets on time, customers want solutions yesterday—and nobody is willing to wait. Time is the most precious resource for businesspeople; consequently, time will always be in short supply. Decisions are often made on the basis of "what we know now" because the situation simply does not allow for delay. As such, you need to constantly seek established data collection and classification systems that can provide reliable outputs quickly. Businesspeople everywhere need to address the increasingly time-starved context within which they work and assess its ramifications.

- **Highly ambiguous situations.** Ambiguity comes in many forms. It can emanate from the nature of competition, the range of competitive tactics employed, key stakeholders' responses in a competitive arena, product and/or process enhancements, consumer responses to competitive tactics, and so on. These types of interjections have been studied by researchers who have recognized that ambiguity can be a potent barrier to competitive imitation and allow for a competitor to sustain an advantage for a longer period.

- **Incrementally received/processed information.** Rarely will you get the information you need in time and in the format you require. The inability of traditional executive information systems to capture, classify, and rank rumors, gossip, grapevine data, and knowledge held by employees out in the field means that you may lack the kind of primary source information that has always been the "jewel in the crown" element that makes analysis so valuable.

Excellent analysis is the key to successful business insights, and good insights can provide high-value, anticipatory decision support capability in contemporary enterprises. Insight about customers, competitors, potential partners, suppliers, and other influential stakeholders is a company's first—and often only—line of offense or defense. Maintaining this capability into the future requires business executives to exploit every opportunity to deliver analysis that is persuasive, relevant, timely, perceptive, and actionable.

Analytical outputs must provide the decision-making process with the essential insight needed to preserve an organization's competitiveness and highlight early warning signs of market changes. We expect that this book will provide you with some helpful guidance and assistance in delivering improved insights to support your organization's competitive endeavors and in achieving market sense-making objectives.

2

The Analysis Process

Analysis is the ugly duckling of effective management. Few management authors write about analysis, not many people want to talk about it, and even fewer people claim to be expert at it. Just compare the commercial availability and visibility of data analysis to data collection. Data collectors are found on every street corner, data collection methods are common and available to most takers, and data collection agencies are plentiful. Don't believe us? Go to your local library, search the Internet, or read the commercial ads in your industry magazines.

Why then has analysis gotten the bad rap? We think there are a number of reasons that can potentially explain why analysis is not among the most popular topics of discussion at the executive dinner table. Apart from some of the reasons we identified in Chapter 1, "Business Management and the Role of Analysis":

1. **Analysis is hard to do for most people.** As in nature, people tend to prefer taking the path of least resistance when it comes to putting forth effort or expending energy. In today's turbo-charged digital world, it is far easier to collect a lot of data than it is to figure out what to do with it. This helps explain why one of the fastest growing industries globally during the past decade has been digital storage.

2. **Few people have publicly recognized or established analysis expertise.** Even those who do may not necessarily be

able to "teach" or disseminate how to do it. Analysis skills can be developed over time as one grows in experience and knowledge.

3. **There are few frameworks for understanding how the analysis component can be managed as an integral part of the decision-making process.** Few individuals can thoughtfully explain how analysis can be successfully managed according to the "three E's"—efficiency, effectiveness, and efficacy. Kind of like riding a bicycle; many people just jump on and ride, but they cannot explain how they perform it to the novice or the four-year-old child hoping to get rid of his training wheels.

It is our view and the findings of several large-scale business surveys that data collection is managed far more successfully than analysis. We see a number of prevalent symptoms that suggest why analysis is not managed properly:

1. **Tool rut.** Like the man who has a hammer and begins to think everything he sees looks like a nail, people keep using the same tools over and over again. We describe this tendency to overuse the same tools as being in the "tool rut." This is counter to the principle that in addressing the complexity of this ever-changing world, businesspeople need to look at numerous models to provide value.

2. **B-school recipe.** Many individuals charged with doing analysis come out of MBA programs where they have been offered tried-and-true recipes from instructors with financial and management accounting backgrounds. Strategy and competitive analysis are as different from accounting analysis as strategy is from accounting.

3. **Ratio blinders.** Most businesspeople do analysis based on historical data and financial ratios. This can at best only provide comparison and tell them the size of the gap (the *"what"*) between two organizations on a particular data point or data set. It

does not help explain the reasons for *why* the gap exists or *how* to close it.

4. **Convenience shopping.** Individuals frequently do analysis on the basis of the data they happen to have as opposed to the data they *should* have. Because they have certain data at their disposal, they use the analytical technique that suits the data rather than focus the analysis on their questions and/or the insights actually required. This is especially true when accountants are asked to do analysis and they provide outputs that only reflect financial manipulations.

As mentioned in Chapter 1, "Business Management and the Role of Analysis," this is a book about analysis, and we do know that using this term often makes most businesspeople we advise and teach uncomfortable, particularly when we get past the smoke-and-mirrors level at which most people talk.

With the pace of change in today's global competitive environment, organizations are constantly repositioning themselves so as to stay ahead of or to make ground up on their competition. As a result, organizations have a need to better understand and make sense of their environments and of their own evolving and dynamic positions within them. This is the primary objective underlying the process of analysis.

Analysis is without a doubt one of the more difficult and critical roles a manager is called upon to perform. Although great strides have been made in recent years in terms of planning projects and collecting data as mentioned here, the same cannot be said for analysis.

As with the type of research formally taught to scientists, the analysis process can be viewed as holding much in common with the scientific method. Analysts observe certain events, persons, or actions; develop a proposition or hypothesis that describes/explains what they have observed; and then use the hypothesis to make predictions about what may subsequently occur. These predictions can then be further assessed through additional observations or data, and the hypotheses can be modified based on the results.

As identified earlier, business management involves all aspects of a business. It requires a knowledge and understanding of the environmental impacts on an organization to ensure that correct decisions are made and taken. It is not only just about looking at best fit but also of taking into account the needs of different stakeholders and diagnosing factors required to create a good outcome.

So how do you formulate strategies and ensure they are the right ones? It is only through the careful collection, examination, and evaluation of the facts that appropriate alternatives can be weighed in light of organizational resources and requirements.

In today's world of information overload, collection of data or information is not, in our opinion, the key issue. Instead, it is the examination and evaluation of the information through analysis that is the key to defining appropriate strategies and decisions. This process requires skill, time, and effort. While most organizations gather some forms of competitive information, surprisingly few formally analyze it and integrate the results into their ongoing business decision-making and strategy development processes.

What Is Analysis?

When we use the word *analysis*, we mean the separation of the whole into its constituent parts to understand each part's value, kind, quantity, or quality. It is not just about reasoning from the universal or general to the particular; nor is it about summarizing the information collected. It is about breaking down an issue into its parts. Today's executive mindset says that every organization needs to have at least some professionals who are actively engaged in evaluating and examining each part.

How does one engage in evaluating and examining each part?

Analysis is a multifaceted, multidisciplinary combination of scientific and nonscientific processes by which an individual interprets the data or information to provide meaningful insights. It is used to derive correlations, evaluate trends and patterns, identify performance gaps, and above all to identify and evaluate opportunities available to organizations. Analysis answers that critical "so what?" question about the data we gather and brings insight to bear directly on the decision-making process.

Effective analysis requires experience, good inputs, intuition, models, and some would argue, even a dash of good luck. It requires constantly varying combinations of art and science, common sense and informed models, and intuition and instruction.

The reason we do analysis is that, although there may be plenty of information around, the issues being analyzed are often quite complex, and the overall reality of the situation may not be all that obvious at first glance.

Figure 2.1 identifies a generic process to analysis.

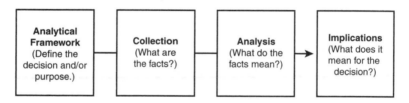

Figure 2.1   A generic approach to analysis

As a process, analysis depends upon raw data. However, not just any data will lead to effective analysis. The data collected and used to respond to your requirements needs to be assessed for its accuracy and reliability.

You need to be aware that understanding accuracy means recognizing that not all data is of equal quality. Some data may be excellent, some marginal, some may be bad, and some might even be intended to deceive. Your data sources must be assessed to know whether input data is accurate and reliable.

Sources often have different reasons for supplying data. Knowing the reason that lies under an individual or group's data is important in establishing the fit of these purposes for analysis. Some data sources can be notorious for projecting biases on to data sets. For example, advocacy groups that have policy agendas are often prejudiced in the data they provide to policy makers, sometimes leaving out data that counters their positions while over-emphasizing data in support of their positions. As you can appreciate, effective analysis relies on effective data collection.

Apart from good data collection, there is no "one best way" to perform analysis. We have met our share of individuals who have wanted to drink from the mythical "analysis spring." The mythical spring, more popularly known as software, that will reliably do the analysis task, does not exist, and we strongly doubt that it ever will. Despite this, we do believe it is possible to improve your expertise in this process by attending to such things as

- How to select and sort data and informational inputs (that is, the "need to know" from the "nice to know" or "who cares about knowing" items)
- What analytical technique to apply to a particular need
- What must be understood in effectively informing organizational actions and decisions

Good analysis simply comes from ongoing practice. The more you practice the techniques in this book, the better you will be able to undertake each technique, and the better will be the quality of your insights.

Whether the application of the analytical techniques can achieve their potential usefulness depends on a number of factors. Based on our experience and understanding of the application of these techniques, there are several warnings to be heeded in performing formal analysis.

First, many organizations have utilized formal methods as a means of taking "superficial shortcuts" to management decision making. The methods we describe in this book are all based on empirical research and are supported by solid theory developed across a range of managerial disciplines. By presenting the methods individually and in a simplified fashion as we have in this book, we do not mean to suggest that their application can lead to "magic bullet" answers.

Second, there is no one right analytical tool for every situation. The depth and complexity of analysis is dependent upon the business situation and your needs. It is important that you understand your needs clearly first. No method by itself will provide all the answers needed by executives intent on improving their competitiveness. Analytical techniques nearly always have to be used for specific purposes and in various combinations to obtain optimal results.

Third, you should be wary of becoming overly reliant on a small number of techniques. This is especially prevalent with inexperienced analysts and can happen for a few main reasons, including

- Generating positive results from the application of a particular technique
- Developing a level of comfort with using the technique
- Having convenient data that supports the application of a particular technique

The use of the techniques as described in this book might lead you to circumvent the quality and/or quantity of analysis necessary for formulating and implementing effective competitive strategy for a number of reasons. For example, our experience suggests that it is far too easy to draw incorrect conclusions from incomplete or defective data with a number of these techniques. As mentioned earlier the quality of the data is critical to the effective delivery of analytical outputs.

You should also note that in spite of the presence of a very broad range of analytical techniques, a few of which we describe in this book, some organizations may still adopt poor decisions. Researchers have identified a variety of common cognitive biases that can enter into the process of analysis. These include

- **Escalating commitment.** This is where executives commit more and more resources to a project even when they receive evidence that it is failing. The more rational move would be to "cut one's losses and run," but rationality is often overcome in these cases by feelings of personal responsibility, an inability to admit one's error, or a failure to acknowledge changes in the assumptions that supported the initial decision.

- **"Groupthink."** This occurs when a group of decision makers (for example, a senior management team) embarks on a poorly determined course of action without thoroughly questioning the underlying assumptions of the decision. It is often based on an emotional rather than an objective assessment of the appropriate course of action and is most prevalent in organizations with strong leadership and cultures.

- **Illusion of control.** This is an individual's tendency to overestimate her ability to control events. For example, someone who has had an ongoing string of picking winning lottery tickets might come to think that they are better "pickers" than they truly are. This is often the result of overconfidence, and senior executives have been shown to be particularly prone to this bias.

- **The prior hypothesis bias.** Individuals who have strong beliefs about the relationships between variables tend to make decisions on the basis of these beliefs even when presented with analytical evidence that contradicts them. Additionally, these individuals often seek and use data only when it confirms their beliefs while ignoring data that contradicts them. In strategic terms, this may happen when the top executive has a strong belief that the organization's existing strategy makes sense and continues to pursue it despite the evidence that shows it is inappropriate.

- **Simplification.** This is where individuals use simple examples to make sense out of not so simple problems. Oversimplifying complex problems is dangerous and can mislead an organization into making bad decisions. This is one of the key cautions we make in applying the techniques contained in this book.

- **Representativeness.** This is a bias that violates the statistical law of large numbers in that individuals often display a tendency to generalize from small samples (such as their experience) to explain a larger phenomena or population.

The existence of these biases raises questions as to the analytical process and its purpose and outcomes. People in organizations often tend to collect more information than strictly necessary for decision making, partly to influence others and partly to be seen as "rational." In other words, analysis is often used not just for objective decision making but also for political purposes.

In fact, formal analysis would be less necessary if people could execute their decisions themselves and nobody had to convince anybody of anything.

Because of these issues and related problems, these techniques should never be used to circumvent the strategic thinking necessary to gain a thorough understanding of an organization's business and competitive environment today or where it should be in the future. They will help improve strategic thinking but are not a replacement for it.

What does it take to successfully perform analysis? There are a number of "competencies" that someone undertaking analysis should demonstrate. One of the better summaries of these competencies comes from the Society of Competitive Intelligence Professionals (SCIP) who suggests the following:

- Recognize the interaction between the collection and analysis stages.
- Use creativity.
- Employ both deductive and inductive reasoning.
- Use alternative thinking.
- Understand the basic analytical models.
- Introduce exciting and attractive models to elicit the discovery notion of analysis rather than the dry, research approach.

- Know when and why to use the various analysis tools.
- Recognize the inevitable existence of gaps and blind spots.
- Know when to cease analyzing so as to avoid analysis paralysis.

There are literally hundreds of strategic, tactical, and operational analysis techniques that we could have included in this book. Instead, we have extensively reviewed the literature in the field, considered survey research and our own experiences in determining those we view as potentially being the most applicable across a broad range of applications in the analysis process.

As outlined in Chapter 1, this book examines ten so-called "classic" techniques involved in analyzing business and competitive data and information including environmental analysis, industry analysis, competitor analysis, and organizational analysis models. It will help any businessperson to draw effective conclusions from limited data and to put together information that does not often fit together at first glance.

You should also be alert to the fact that any listing of techniques is bound to run into a variety of problems of semantics and definitional confusion. Some of the techniques included in this book are known by multiple names. This might have occurred because the technique came to be associated with a particular originating organization (for example, the BCG matrix), a particular author (Porter's Five Forces model is an example), or has retained a generic nomenclature (perhaps competitor analysis). We recognize that some of the techniques included in this book have seen modifications in use over the years or are derivatives of other closely related techniques. In all cases, we have tried to include and describe the most popularly known versions of the techniques as opposed to all of a technique's possible derivatives. We have tried to alert you to where there is overlap between techniques by referring you to the supporting techniques within the text.

We must also note that it is not our intention to "invent a new wheel" when it comes to the analytical techniques. The techniques included herein all have a history. This book's techniques have been and are in use in real organizations—they do not exist just in theory.

Many of the techniques included in this book were conceptualized by leading economists, financial and cost accountants, futurists, business professors, consultants, and other insightful practitioners or theoreticians. They often developed their ideas in an effort to solve pressing analytical problems that they faced. We are grateful to these individuals for enlightening our understanding of strategic and competitive analysis. We make a sincere attempt to acknowledge the originators of these techniques in the book. Nevertheless, there are times when accurately making this acknowledgement can be difficult, such as when the technique (for example, SWOT) was quickly and widely accepted and came to form the commonly held body of knowledge underlying organizational decision making.

Part
II

Analysis Tools

Chapter 3 BCG Growth/Share Portfolio Matrix 29

Chapter 4 Competitor Analysis 49

Chapter 5 Financial Ratio and Statement Analysis 67

Chapter 6 Five Forces Industry Analysis 95

Chapter 7 Issue Analysis 111

Chapter 8 Political Risk Analysis 131

Chapter 9 Scenario Analysis 151

Chapter 10 Macroenvironmental (STEEP/PEST) Analysis 169

Chapter 11 SWOT Analysis 183

Chapter 12 Value Chain Analysis 199

3

BCG Growth/Share Portfolio Matrix

Description and Purpose

Portfolio planning models are designed to help the analyst better understand the attractiveness or potential of a portfolio of distinct business units in a multi-unit business. They developed from two areas: the planning department at General Electric (GE) and the Boston Consulting Group (BCG). GE is generally credited with being the first to present a comprehensive portfolio matrix in the early 1960s.

Shortly after the initial developments at GE, BCG took the business world by storm with its introduction of its Growth/Share Portfolio matrix (BCG matrix). Its intuitive appeal and vivid imagery combined with the appearance of good quantitative analysis caught the interest of many strategic planners searching for a legitimate tool to manage diversified multi-unit corporate strategy.

The BCG matrix was designed to help managers of multiproduct, multimarket, multinational businesses assess their corporate level strategy by

- Providing them with an analytical framework to determine the optimal product or business portfolio
- Prescribing a set of strategies to guide resource allocation across the portfolio

- Providing them with a framework for analyzing competing business portfolios

The BCG matrix allows a multibusiness company to evaluate the merits of its individual business units or business lines to determine appropriate market strategies for each business. The business portfolios are evaluated using a common measuring stick based on the attractiveness of the industry in which they compete and their relative competitive position. Generic strategies are then recommended depending on the position of the individual business unit or line in the portfolio matrix.

Crafting a fit between the organization's goals, capabilities, and the environment in which it operates is at the core of strategic planning. The tactical delivery of strategic planning is the allocation of resources to competing internal opportunities. This is a challenging task for focused companies, but it can quickly spiral into unmanageable complexity for a diversified company.

The BCG matrix integrated two previously established management theories: the experience curve and the product life cycle.

Link to the Experience Curve

BCG found that per unit costs often decrease as output levels increase due to the impact of experience. Experience is composed of three functions: learning, specialization, and scale.

The *learning function* shows that anyone doing a job learns to do it better over time.

The *specialization function* shows that by dividing jobs into individual tasks, each employee's experience with the task increases, and costs decline because of the increased learning.

The *scale function* suggests that the capital costs required to finance additional capacity diminish as that capacity grows.

The sequential impact of these three functions on profitability is shown in Figure 3.1.

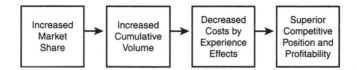

Figure 3.1 Experience curve sequence

Based on this logical sequence, a major strategic implication was drawn from experience curve theory: The company capturing the largest market share achieves the highest accumulated volume, achieving a superior competitive position due to cost reductions from the experience curve effect.

Link to the Product Life Cycle

The other building block of the BCG growth matrix was the well-established concept of the product life cycle (PLC). The product life cycle was selected as the natural complement to the experience curve based on the following chain of logic.

If market share is the surest road to higher accumulated volumes and subsequent lower costs/higher profitability, then the company's resources are best spent pursuing high growth markets.

The surest route to maximize total company profitability is to maximize market share across the strategic business unit (SBU) or business line (SBL) portfolio. The best way to accomplish this is to transfer profits or resources away from the mature and declining products to introductory and growth products of the PLC. The relevant assumptions of the PLC are twofold:

- Market share is easier to secure in high-growth markets because competitive retaliation is less severe when it is secured through new growth instead of taking it from competitors. It is also easier to secure because new consumers or users have lower branding preference relative to experienced ones.

- Products in the mature stage of the life cycle generate excess cash, whereas products in the growth stage require or absorb more cash.

Combining the Experience Curve and the Product Life Cycle

The BCG matrix in Figure 3.2 is the result of the integration of experience curve and PLC theory.

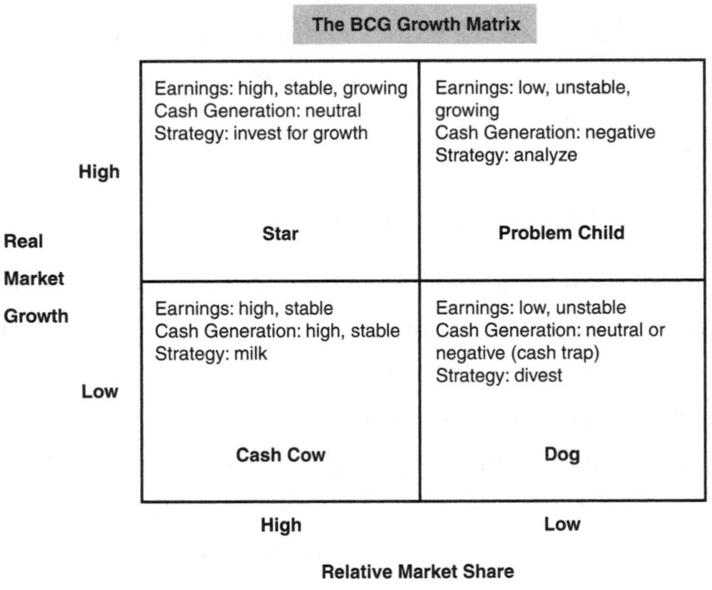

The BCG Growth Matrix

High	Earnings: high, stable, growing Cash Generation: neutral Strategy: invest for growth **Star**	Earnings: low, unstable, growing Cash Generation: negative Strategy: analyze **Problem Child**
Low	Earnings: high, stable Cash Generation: high, stable Strategy: milk **Cash Cow**	Earnings: low, unstable Cash Generation: neutral or negative (cash trap) Strategy: divest **Dog**
	High	**Low**

Real Market Growth (vertical axis)

Relative Market Share (horizontal axis)

Figure 3.2   BCG growth matrix

The BCG matrix plots market attractiveness (measured by market growth as derived from PLC theory) and competitive position (measured by market share as derived from experience curve theory) to compare the situation of different products and/or SBUs. Market attractiveness is measured by the industry's growth rate, whereas competitive position is measured by the business unit's market share relative to that of its largest competitor in the industry (as opposed to the market as a whole). For example, if a business unit has a market share of 20 percent and its largest competitor has a market share of 40 percent, then the business unit's relative market share is 0.5. The purpose of this comparison is to define an appropriate market strategy for each business unit.

The overall strategy of the multibusiness company, as suggested by the BCG matrix, is to maximize market share in as many high-growth markets for as many SBUs/SBLs as possible. The upper limit of this possibility is limited by cash flow because the model assumes an internal cash balance between cash uses and cash generation. Hence, the strategic goal for senior executives is to allocate limited cash resources across the business units or lines to maximize company profitability.

Each quadrant in the BCG matrix offers generic strategies to achieve maximum profitability under this constraint.

Stars—High Growth Rate, High Market Share

The high growth rate of stars requires a heavy cash investment. Their strong market share position infers that stars move furthermost along the experience curve. Therefore, stars should soon develop high margins, resulting in potentially strong cash flows in the near future and, hence, a sustainable cash position. Application of the BCG matrix presumes that stars will eventually become cash cows. It recommends that if stars are cash-deficient, they should be supported with the investment necessary to maintain their market share; and if they are cash providers, the surplus should be reinvested.

Cash Cows—Low Growth Rate, High Market Share

Products or SBUs in mature markets require lower cash investments and, therefore, will provide cash flow from which to finance businesses in other more promising quadrants. The BCG matrix suggests that cash cows be "milked" by a strategy that only invests to maintain their current positions. Excess cash flow should be rein-vested in either stars or selected problem children.

Dogs—Low Growth Rate, Low Market Share

The low growth rate of dogs infers that increasing their market share will be a costly proposition. Additionally, their low market share implies an uncompetitive cost structure by virtue of their inferior position on the experience curve. Hence, dogs are unprofitable and usually require heavy cash investments just to maintain their low market share. An application of the BCG matrix recommends three options for dogs:

- They can become profitable with a focused strategy on a specific desired niche or segment.
- Any further investment can be withheld while "milking" them for any cash that they can still generate.
- They can be divested or slowly put to sleep.

Problem Children—High Growth Rate, Low Market Share

The high growth rate of problem children requires a heavy cash investment. An intensifying factor is their low market share, which implies an uncompetitive cost structure by virtue of their inferior position on the experience curve. As the maturity stage sets in, the problem child follows one of two paths on the matrix:

- If market share cannot be grown, the problem child will become a dog.
- Alternately, if market share can be increased by a high enough amount, the problem child will be exalted into star status and eventually become a cash cow.

The BCG matrix recommends that the most promising problem children should receive cash investments to increase their market share, but those problem children with dismal prospects should not receive further cash investment.

The integration of these classifications and their requisite strategies are shown in Figure 3.3. (The numbers indicate strategic priority.)

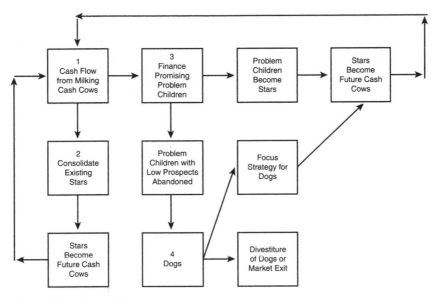

Figure 3.3 Overall strategic sequence

Strengths

The simplicity of the BCG matrix may be its greatest strength. It presents a great deal of information in one diagram; the complexities of a multibusiness strategy are seemingly captured in an accessible format. Many other management tools cannot match the depth and breadth of information that this growth/share matrix offers in one concise view. Its straightforwardness allows it to be used easily and quickly to identify areas for further in-depth analysis.

The BCG matrix challenged the status quo that internal investment should be directed on the basis of past performance or should reward managers for past performance. In some respects, the portfolio approach fosters a mindset focused on future demand.

It additionally assists with areas such as the following:

- **Trend analysis.** Changes in the relative SBU markets can be detected easily through the use of multiperiod matrices.

- **Competitive analysis.** Determining the strategic progress of competitor companies can be easily facilitated by plotting a time series of competitor matrices.

- **Easy to communicate.** The matrix and the resulting recommendations are easy for decision makers to understand.

- **Challenges existing management philosophy.** One of the main strengths of portfolio analysis is the change in perspective that it induces in the minds of its users. It recognizes that corporate strategy must be an integration of individual business strategy at the business unit level. This was an improvement on the preceding mindset that tended to apply blanket strategies across the entire multi-unit company and neglected the differences across the various product markets in which it operated. The BCG portfolio approach heightens management's sensitivity by combining corporate level and business level strategy.

Weaknesses

BCG matrix has several limitations. The experience curve link to the BCG matrix may not be relevant to the competitive parameters of a particular product market. Relative market share is not necessarily a good proxy for competitive position (that is, there is not a clear or singular relationship between market share and profitability in all industries).

High market share is not necessarily more profitable than low market share. Many profitable companies have demonstrated that competition in low growth mature markets should not be categorically ruled out as a strategic option. Similarly, the emphasis on market dominance is being constantly challenged by successful niche players who specialize in product or service differentiation.

Market share is assumed to be a dependent variable, whereas market growth is assumed to be an independent variable. This is not necessarily correct. The assumption that market growth rate is a variable beyond the control of management confuses the cause and effect sequence of effective strategy—strategy should lead to growth rather than growth leading to strategy.

The BCG matrix assumes that investment opportunities inside a company are superior to investment opportunities outside the company. The emergence of advanced capital markets, coupled with the difficulty of managing diversity in the absence of specific market knowledge, suggests that portfolio management has become less useful. It is quite possible that increasing dividends or investing surplus cash cow funds in money markets offers a higher rate of return than investing internally in stars and problem children.

Strategic business units sometimes cannot be unambiguously defined. The nature of SBUs with regard to their inter-relatedness (such as, joint costs, synergy, demand, and interdependencies) makes the positioning on the matrix a fruitless exercise in classification.

The characteristics of the product market influence the strategic recommendations offered by the BCG matrix. There is significant room for error in applying the tradeoff between operational breadth (to include competitive experience effects), and depth (to allow for meaningful segmentation).

Often, it is valuable for a company to retain dogs to maintain a portfolio of strategic options, such as supply security, a source of competitive intelligence, and escape from the onset of entry barriers in certain industries. The benefits of strategic flexibility may supercede profitability, at least for a designated period of time. For example, a strict application of portfolio theory would suggest that most car dealerships would be wise to divest their new car business; however, new car sales are often an important driver for the highly lucrative service segment.

Given that the BCG growth matrix only incorporates the competitive threat to market share from the most dominant competitor, there is a risk of being blindsided. A rapidly rising competitor may not show up on the BCG radar until it has gained enough market share to become a dominant player in the market.

A further source of bias may be the selection of data and definition by managers seeking to achieve a star label for their particular management domains. The unintended consequences of the BCG matrix may be "politics" and game playing around these subjective analytical parameters.

While the BCG matrix remains an impressive conceptual framework, it should be primarily used as a starting point for subsequent analysis. When done in conjunction with other analytical tools and techniques, it can help provide a holistic approach to corporate strategy development.

How to Do It

True to its systematic nature, the process for using the BCG matrix is sequential and can be generalized into the following steps.

Step 1: Divide the Company into its SBUs or Business Product Lines/Segments

Divide the company into its economically distinct product market segments or around specific business units. Take care with this first step because the business line's position on the matrix—and hence the strategic recommendations of the model—depend in large part on this initial definition of the product. You are trying to find units that have an established and separate Profit and Loss (P&L) or budgeting profile.

Common segmentation criteria include similar situational or behavioral characteristics, a discontinuity in growth rates, share patterns, distribution patterns, cross elasticity of substitute products, geography, interdependent prices, similar competition, similar customers served and/or a potential for shared experience. A common rule of thumb is that a management team can only realistically manage strategies for approximately 30 different business lines—anything beyond this number becomes unmanageable and counter-productive. As you might imagine, many management teams have struggled with far less than this number!

A great deal of judgment is thus required to determine the extent of segmentation within the product market definition. A wide enough scope must be maintained to correctly incorporate competitive opportunities and threats from areas outside of the traditional or intuitive boundaries. Conversely, the definition of an SBU or strategic business line (SBL) must be narrow enough to allow for distinctions fine enough to make the analysis operational. Despite the difficulty of properly defining the individual business lines or units, this process of analysis often offers important strategic insights of its own accord.

Step 2: Measure the Growth Rate of each SBU or SBL Market

A useful percentage growth formula for measuring the market growth rate is

$$\text{Market Growth Rate, Year}_x = \frac{[\text{Market Size, Year}_x] - [\text{Market Size, Year}_{x-1}]}{\text{Market Size, Year}_{x-1}} \times 100$$

Step 3: Measure the Relative Market Share of Each SBU or SBL

Contrary to the formula in Step 2, relative market share is not measured in percentage terms, but as a ratio of the business unit's or business line's market share versus that of its largest competitor.

$$\text{SBU Relative Market Share, Year}_x = \frac{\text{SBU Sales, Year}_x}{\text{Largest Competitor's Sales, Year}_x}$$

For example, a market share ratio of 2 shows that the SBU has a relative market share twice that of its next leading competitor. Alternately, a ratio of 0.5 shows that the SBU has a relative market share that is half of that of its leading competitor. Note that normally an SBU will have more than one product, making the use of a weighted average of the individual product growth rates a suitable technique. Either nominal or real sales data may be used. You want an accurate estimate of relative market share; however, you do not need two decimal levels of precision in generating the ratio!

Step 4: Position Each SBU or SBL Along the Matrix Dimensions

Plotting on the Vertical Axis—Market Growth Rate

Simply plot the percentages on the vertical axis. Next, draw a threshold point to distinguish SBUs or SBLs that are experiencing fast growth from those that are gaining market share slowly. The BCG matrix uses the average growth rate for the market as this horizontal line of demarcation. Alternately, a corporate target may be used to define this threshold. Consistent with the product life cycle, products that lie above this line are considered to be in the growth stage. Products or business lines below this line are considered to be in either the maturity or decline stage of the product life cycle.

Plotting on the Horizontal Axis—Relative Market Share

Experience curve theory asserts that market share is related to total accumulated volume, which is the major factor driving down costs through the experience curve effect. Plot relative market share on a semi-log scale. A *semi-log graph* or *semi-log plot* is a way of visualizing data that is changing with an exponential relationship. One axis is plotted on a logarithmic scale.

A cut-off point also needs to be established on the horizontal axis with regard to both high and low market share. The BCG matrix recommends this vertical line of demarcation to be a relative market share of 1.0. Any relative market share to the right of 1.0 indicates the threshold of competitive strength in that market.

Plot Contribution Bubbles

The two cut-off points (high versus low growth and high versus low market share) allow the graph to be divided into the characteristic four quadrants of the BCG matrix. Plotting the growth rate versus relative market share will only give pinpoint locations on the matrix. A helpful technique is to plot bubbles around these points to indicate the relative size of each SBU/SBL in terms of its contribution to total company sales or profitability.

$$\text{Relative Size of Bubble} = \frac{(\text{SBU Sales or Profitability})}{\text{Total Firm Sales or Profitability}}$$

Sales volume is generally a preferred basis for determining the size of the bubbles for several reasons: It is easier to make a comparison to competition (see Step 5), competitor profit figures by SBU/SBL are difficult to obtain, and internal profit figures are often distorted by arbitrary allocations. Each bubble should also be labeled using a common convention, such as numerical or alphabetical order for further referencing.

Upon determining each unit's placement within the matrix, the following predictions can be made: the size, stability, and growth potential of the future earnings of each business unit or line and the cash flow that each business should provide.

The intermediate analytical product of Steps 1 through 4 should look similar to the graph displayed in Figure 3.4.

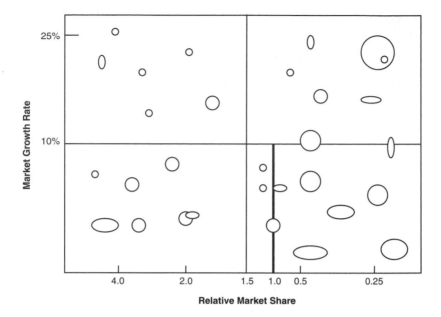

Figure 3.4   Matrix graph

Step 5: Construct a Matrix for All Competitors

Repeat Steps 1 through 4 to construct matrices for competitor business units or product lines. This will help to give the analysis an external focus on the competitive environment.

Step 6: Assign Optimal Generic Strategies to Each Business Unit or Product Line

Table 3.1 summarizes the appropriate strategies recommended by an application of the BCG matrix after the SBUs/SBLs have been positioned in the matrix. Basically, the strategies can be summarized by the following modes of action: divest the dogs; milk the cash cows; invest in the stars; and analyze the problem child to determine whether it can be grown into a star or will degenerate into a dog.

TABLE 3.1   Strategies for BCG Matrix

Business Category	Market Share Thrust	Business Profitability	Investment Required	Net Cash Flow
Stars	Hold/Increase	High	High	Around zero or slightly negative
Cash Cows	Hold	High	Low	Highly positive
Problem Child (a)	Increase	None or negative	Very high	Highly negative
Problem Child (b)	Harvest/ Divest	Low or negative	Do not invest	Positive
Dogs	Harvest/ Divest	Low or negative	Do not invest	Positive

Adapted from Arnoldo Hax and N.S., "The Use of the Growth Share Matrix in Strategic Planning," *Interfaces*, February 1983, 46–60.

Step 7: Further Disaggregate the Analysis

The matrix approach can be further defined to map out the relative positions of the composite products within each business. This might help with the tactical implementation of Step 6.

Step 8: Introduce Analytical Dynamics

Steps 1 through 7 result in a static analysis. Two analytical tools can be introduced at this stage to incorporate historical market evolution and sustainable growth rate, as follows.

Construct a Share Momentum Graph

The purpose of a share momentum graph is to plot long-term market growth versus long-term sales to detect which SBUs/SBLs are losing market share despite growing sales. This tool is easy to apply because it uses the same data as the matrix. It serves to highlight important distinctions that may be overlooked by only using the BCG matrix (see Figure 3.5).

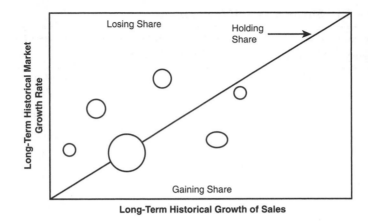

Figure 3.5   Share momentum graph
Adapted from Arnoldo Hax and N.S., "The Use of the Growth Share Matrix in Strategic Planning," *Interfaces*, February 1983, 52.

Sustainable Growth Rate Analysis

Introduced during the high inflationary era of the 1970s, the BCG matrix assumed that the company's growth would be internally financed. In a lower inflation environment, the sustainable growth rate formula can be used to determine the maximum rate of growth without increasing equity. It is a helpful way to integrate financial strategy with the BCG matrix.

$g = p \times [\text{ROA} = \text{D/E}(\text{ROA} - i)]$ where
g = upper limit on sustainable growth
p = percentage of earnings retained
ROA = tax adjusted return on assets
D = total debt
E = total equity
i = tax adjusted cost of debt

Step 9: Iteration

Repeating Steps 1 through 8 serves two strategic purposes: strategic evaluation and competitive analysis.

Strategic Evaluation

The success of the chosen strategies over time can be graphically displayed by overlaying a time series matrix chart to determine if a business unit or business product lines are moving into their desired positions on the matrix. An optimal result would show that problem children increase in both market share and market growth rate to become stars; stars decrease in market growth rate but sustain market share to become cash cows; dogs are either divested or moved into the problem child or star quadrants; and cash cows exhibit stable positions.

Competitive Analysis

The progress of rival companies can be monitored by repeating this process with a time series of matrix graphs compiled of competitors and constructing an updated share momentum graph for competitors. Competitive threats and opportunities may reveal themselves with these tools. It has been suggested that the best competitive analysis within a matrix format is the share momentum graphs (see Figure 3.5) because temporary aberrations will not distort the analysis, and cut-off points may change over time.

Case Study

The Broadband Cable TV Industry

During the first decade in the twenty-first century, it is anticipated that the cable industry will become another access technology in the converging markets of telecommunications, broadcasting, Internet, and e-commerce. The first signs of this new trend started to appear in the late 1990s. Cable TV operators in the United States upgraded their networks and slowly started to add high-speed Internet services. These were seen as an important step to surpass satellite demand.

For millions of people across the globe, television brings news, entertainment, and educational programs into their homes. Many people get their TV signals now from cable television (CATV) because it provides a clearer picture and more channels. Many people who have cable TV can now also get a high-speed connection (broadband) to the Internet from their cable providers.

Despite the apparent growth opportunities, the broadband cable industry has experienced financial difficulty. As part of a study to examine the status and strategies of this industry on a worldwide basis, a BCG matrix was used to identify the nature of the products offered. The positioning of the "products" of the broadband cable industry into a BCG matrix was undertaken, with the following results identified in Figure 3.6.

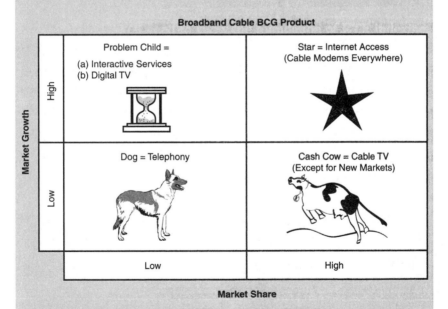

Figure 3.6   Broadband cable BCG product portfolio

From this BCG matrix, the following conclusions could be drawn at a global level:

- The telephony services—the dog—should be reviewed and consideration be given as to whether or not to discontinue them.

- The cable TV service—the cash cow—should be managed on a cost-conscious basis to deliver the maximum positive cash flow.

- The cash flow from the cable TV service would be used to support the continued growth of the Internet access service—the star—and to promote the development of the new interactive services—the problem child—any one of which could possibly become the growth star of the future.

- Interactive services— the problem child—is closely coupled with the deployment of digital TV, where the intention is to provide them on a TV set. Otherwise they could be supported through Internet access services using a PC. However, they would then become part of the electronic commerce Internet world, and the ability of the broadband cable company to add value (and thereby derive additional revenue) would be extremely limited.

The fundamental issue of how the choice between TV and PC will be resolved—or more realistically, how the two will be merged within a home network—might well decide the next star service.

Case study adapted from M. McGrail and B. Roberts, "Strategies in the Broadband Cable TV Industry: The Challenges for Management and Technology Innovation," *INFO*, 7(1), Emerald Group Publishing Ltd., 2005, 53–65.

4

Competitor Analysis

Description and Purpose

The purpose of competitor analysis is to provide a comprehensive picture of the strengths and weaknesses of current and potential competitors to identify opportunities and threats for your organization. The four main objectives of competitor analysis are as follows:

- Identify competitors' future plans and strategies
- Predict competitors' likely reactions to competitive initiatives
- Determine the match between a competitor's strategy and its capabilities
- Understand a competitor's inabilities or weaknesses

Professor Michael Porter from Harvard University was one of the first strategists to propose a formal and systematic model to gather information about competitors (see Figure 4.1). This model encourages you to use current and past information about competitors to predict the future strategic moves that a competitor may pursue in response to the company's own strategies, the strategies of other companies in the industry, or broad changes in the competitive environment external to business strategies. This puts you in a superior position to craft both defensive and offensive strategies.

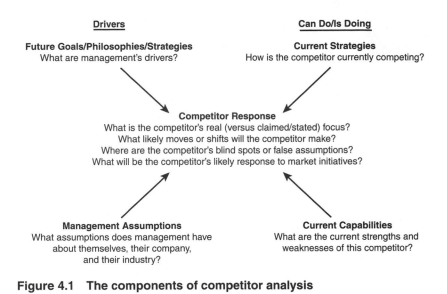

Figure 4.1   The components of competitor analysis

Adapted from Michael E. Porter, *Competitive Strategy: Techniques for Analyzing Industries and Competitors* (New York: The Free Press, 1980).

The rationale for competitor analysis is simple—a superior knowledge of competitors offers a legitimate source of competitive advantage. The essence of competitive advantage consists of offering superior customer value in the company's chosen market. Customer value is defined relative to competitor offerings, making competitor knowledge an intrinsic component of corporate strategy.

Competitor analysis facilitates the objective of achieving superior customer value in three important ways:

- First, it can reveal strategic weaknesses your organization can attempt to exploit in the competitor being studied.
- Second, its proactive stance allows you to anticipate the response of your competitors to your planned strategies, the strategies of other competing companies, and changes in the environment.
- Third, this knowledge can give your company strategic agility.

Offensive strategy can be implemented more quickly to capitalize on your strengths and exploit opportunities. Similarly, defensive strategy can be employed more deftly to counter the threat of competitor companies from exploiting your company's weaknesses.

Clearly, companies practicing systematic and advanced competitor analysis and profiling have a significant advantage. As such, a comprehensive profiling capability is becoming a core competence required for successful business competition.

Strengths

In addition to the advantages just outlined, there are several other related benefits:

- Competitor analysis encourages your company to adopt a confident, aggressive, and proactive position toward competitive strategy and the broader business environment.
- The knowledge provided about competitors allows your company to help shape and define the parameters of strategy rather than react to unexpected competitive sideswipes.
- The inclusive nature of competitor analysis encourages the sharing of insights and perspectives across functional boundaries of the company. Many opportunities are often uncovered that otherwise would have remained hidden.
- It creates an efficient and effective approach to strategy formulation. The relevant, timely, concise, and visually accessible presentation formats of this technique are an excellent vehicle to communicate strategy.

Weaknesses

The primary criticism of competitor analysis relates to the temptation for companies to make it the cornerstone of their competitive strategy. In attempting to become an industry leader, a company will eventually become a follower if it defines leadership too closely in respect to current competitors because

- Comparisons to competitors must always relate to the notion of customer value.

- Constantly referencing a company's strategy to competitors will eventually blind a company to innovative approaches of potential new competitors from *outside* the periphery of the industry who deliver superior customer value. Thus, it is important to keep an eye on potential new competitors from seemingly unrelated sectors and industries.

The copycat nature of outpacing the competition may prevent any competitive advantage from becoming sustainable—companies should focus on generating real customer value, not "me-too" imitation, in their search for profitable innovation.

How to Do It

There are seven steps in the competitor analysis process:

1. Determine who your competitors are.

2. Determine who your potential competitors may be.

3. Decide what information you need about these competitors.

4. Conduct a competitor analysis of the gathered information.

5. Present your insights to decision makers in an appropriate format and in a timely manner.

6. Develop a strategy based on the analysis.

7. Continually monitor competitors and scan for potential competitors.

Steps 1 and 2: Determine Who Your Competitors Are and Who They May Be in the Future

The first two steps are closely related. Your competitors include those companies that serve the same customer base as you. However, what is your customer base? Is it customers of the same product or customers of the same product category? Ultimately, all companies are competitors in that they are all trying to attract the same discretionary income. Although this last delineation may sound extreme, it underscores the importance of including potential competitors at the beginning of the analysis. Given the factors of industry changes and value chain erosion, it is important to include potential new competitors at the outset to prevent the analysis from becoming too narrowly focused.

There are two ways to define competitors:

- **The traditional method.** More adept at identifying current competitors, this method focuses on defining strategic groups within industries. Strategic groups are closely related companies with relatively similar strategies, occupying similar links on the industry's value chain and sharing similar resource capabilities.

- **The less obvious method.** This focuses on identifying potential new competitors who are not yet visible. They are developing new ways of delivering customer value on new competitive platforms and are often unaware of the companies they will soon supplant. By focusing on customer value and the question, "Which competitors do *your* customers see as *your* major competition?" companies can define potential competitors according to their provision of comparable customer value through different platforms, of products and services. Focus on defining potential competitors based on changing customer tastes and preferences, motivations, product or service deployment, or technological innovation.

Generally, the most valuable sources of information regarding the identification of both current and potential competitors will be your company's own customers, sales staff, marketing representatives, and operations managers—in other words, those who interact the most with customers. Other less valuable sources may be found in industry directories, trade association materials, and other secondary information resources.

Step 3: Decide What Information You Need About These Competitors

Start this step with the internal end user of the output of your analysis—the strategic decision makers within your company. They will be in the best position to itemize exactly what types of competitor information would be most beneficial. To facilitate this objective, focus information gathering on the strategic needs of the decision makers.

Table 4.1 depicts the types and categories of information that may be considered during this stage.

You can get ideas about useful types and sources of information from surveys and benchmarking studies. However, information needs will be largely industry-specific or even company-specific and will change over time.

TABLE 4.1   Typical Categories and Types of Competitor Profile Information

Background Information	Products/Services	Marketing
• Name	• Number of products/ services	• Segmentation strategies
• Location	• Diversity or breadth of product lines	• Branding and image
• Short description		• Probable growth vectors
• History	• Quality, embedded customer value	• Advertising/promotions
• Key events	• Projected new products/services	• Market research capability
• Major transactions		• Customer service emphasis
• Ownership structure	• Current market shares by product and product line	• 4 P parameters—product, price, promotion, place
	• Projected market shares	• Key customers

Human Resources	Operations	Management Profiles
• Quality and skill of personnel	• Manufacturing capacity	• Personality
• Turnover rates	• Ability to mass customize	• Background
• Labor costs	• Cycle time, manufacturing agility, and flexibility	• Motivations, aspirations
• Level of training	• TQM implementation	• Style
• Flexibility	• Overhead costs	• Past successes and failures
• Union relations	• Lean production methods	• Depth of managerial talent

Sociopolitical

- Government contacts
- Stakeholder reputation
- Breadth and depth of portfolio of sociopolitical assets
- Public affairs experience
- Nature of government contracts
- Connections of board members
- Issue and crisis management capacity

Technology

- Process technology
- R&D expertise
- Proprietary technology, patents, copyrights
- Information and communication infrastructure
- Ability to internally innovate
- Access to outside expertise through licensing, alliances, joint ventures

Organizational Structure

- Nature of hierarchy
- Team building
- Cross functionality
- Major ownership
- Cultural alignment

CI Capacity

- Evidence of formal CI capacity
- Reporting relationships
- Profile
- CEO and top management level of support
- Vulnerability
- Integration
- Data gathering and analysis assets

Financial

- Financial statements
- Securities filings
- Absolute and comparative ratio analysis
- Disaggregated ratio analysis
- Cash flow analysis
- Sustainable growth rate
- Stock performance
- Costs

Strategy

- Positioning
- Future plans
- Mission and vision
- Goals, objectives
- Corporate portfolio
- Synergies
- Resources/capabilities
- Core competencies
- Strengths and weaknesses

Customer Value Analysis

- Quality attributes
- Service attributes
- Customer goals and motivations
- Customer types and numbers
- Net worth (benefits minus costs) of ownership

Contrary to intuition, most of the information required for this step already exists inside your company; that is, salespeople, marketing staff, operations, and probably everyone in the company is in possession of valuable nuggets of competitive information. Figuring prominently in these primary sources of competitive information are your company's own customers and suppliers.

Step 4: Conduct a Competitor Analysis of the Gathered Information

Porter's framework depicted in Figure 4.1 can be used as a guide when analyzing the gathered information as follows:

- **Future goals.** Determining the future goals of your competitors will help to forecast their strategies and identify strategies for your company. To understand where a competitor is headed, identify its market share, profitability, and organizational performance. Also try to discover what has been stated by their key spokespeople with regard to their future direction. How do they claim to see themselves operating in the future.

- **Current strategy.** First, determine which of the three strategies (low cost, differentiation, or focus) the company is pursuing. A current strategy may be identified on the basis of both what it says and what it does.

  Next, identify the strategic implications for each functional area of the competitor's business. Functional areas of the business would include marketing, sales, operations, administration, manufacturing, research and development, finance, or personnel.

  What are its stated short-term goals? Start by identifying the differences between its future goals and what it is currently doing. Is there synergy and does it make sense, or will it require a major shift to achieve its long-term goals? Are its short-term activities in line with its future goals? Remember, in the absence of particular forces for change, it can be assumed that a company will continue to compete in the future in the same way it has competed in the past.

- **Capabilities.** Use the information gathered in the *current strategy* previously to identify what the competitor is doing and what it has the capacity to do. This is about capacity, skills, and resources to actually deliver on both its current strategies and future goals. Although a competitor might have announced its strategic intentions, its current capabilities may not enable it to realize them, thus raising questions about the internal thinking of the company.

- **Assumptions.** A competitor's competitive assumptions about itself, the industry, and other competitors yields many useful insights regarding potentially incorrect assumptions or blind spots. Often these blind spots offer competitive opportunities, and this is the crux of the analysis. What assumptions does the competitor hold about its world, and are these reflected in its strategies, both current and future? Assumptions can be identified by the mismatch between capabilities, current strategies, and future goals. On the other hand, a company that has all three areas in sync may be a formidable competitor. However, all companies hold assumptions about the world and the future, and they need to be uncovered.

  The critical issue underlying competitor analysis is in your understanding of the key assumptions made by the competition. These assumptions may allow you to identify fundamental weaknesses in how they compete and how they see their marketplaces. Answering questions such as, "Are they satisfied with this position?" "What are their plans?" and "What are their vulnerabilities?" can provide the necessary understanding to take competitors on.

The four analyses are then integrated into a competitor profile. The purpose is to forecast, with reasonable accuracy, how a competitor will respond to various competitive pressures.

First, determine the offensive position of competitors to predict moves they may initiate. Second, determine the defensive position of competitors to forecast how they might react to various competitive pressures.

In making these determinations, qualitative factors may often outweigh quantitative factors.

Step 5: Present Your Analytical Insights to Decision Makers in an Appropriate Format and in a Timely Manner

Visual depictions are more effective than written reports. Figures 4.2 to 4.4 depict three types of formatting schemes.

- **Comparison grid.** Plot competitor positions (performance, capabilities, key success factor, and so on) on high/low dependent and independent variable cross-hair axes. Depending on the application, the company's performance or industry averages are used as the point of reference. Comparison grids provide good snapshots of relative performance across two competitive parameters (see Figure 4.2).

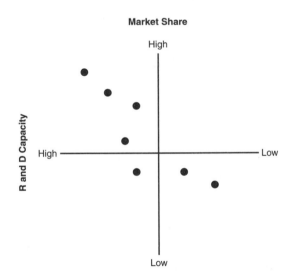

Figure 4.2   Comparison grid

- **Radar chart.** Simple to comprehend yet dense with information, radar charts are often used to communicate profiling analysis. Radar charts are composed of an underlying circle with several points on the circumference representing industry averages around relative competitive parameters. Superimposed over these circles are geometric shapes representing the performance of the company or competitor being analyzed. The

resulting geometric overlay will depict a concise visual of relative performance, whether it be superior or inferior performance (see Figure 4.3).

      Rival A   Industry Average   Analyst's Firm

Figure 4.3   Radar charts

- **Visual competitor strength grid.** Competitor strength grids
  are a simple yet effective way of depicting the relative superiority between competitor companies along any number of competitive parameters. By assigning a spectrum of colors (or
  symbols) to represent relative competitive inferiority, parity,
  and superiority, the graph depicts the spectrum of relative competitive advantage among competitors (see Table 4.2).

**TABLE 4.2   Visual competitor strength grid (for Pizza Delivery
Restaurants in Southern Ontario)**

KSF		Armando's	Domino's	Little Caesar's	Pizza Hut	Pizza King	Pizza Pizza
1	Breadth of Product Offering	<	>	<	★	•	>
2	Geographic Coverage	•	★	>	>	<	<
3	Name Recognition	•	★	>	>	<	<
4	Product Quality	★	<	•	<	>	>
5	Production & Delivery Reliability	<	>	★	>	•	<
6	Supply Chain Management	<	>	★	>	•	<

Guide: ★ Best in class | > Above average | < Below average | • Worst in class

These charts and similar visual depictions will facilitate brainstorming sessions during the strategy development process.

Given the rapidity of environmental and competitive change, competitor intelligence has value only if it is received in a timely fashion by the relevant strategic decision makers. In this respect, timeliness and relevance supersede complete accuracy.

Step 6: Develop Strategy Based on the Analysis

At this point, competitor profiles are used to develop strategy around several relevant competitive considerations, such as

- Determining the probable rules of engagement within that strategic position
- Choosing the arena or scope of engagement—where, how, and against whom your company will compete
- Developing a strategy that leverages your company's strengths, exploits competitors' weaknesses, neutralizes competitive threats, and defends against weaknesses

Choose strategies that will force competitors to make costly strategic trade-offs, should they decide to impinge on your strategy.

Step 7: Continually Monitor Competitors and Scan for Potential Competitors

Always assume that competitors are simultaneously performing similar analysis on your company. This is reason enough to engage in continual monitoring. Volatile markets, hyper-competition, industry migration, and decoupling value chains give ample rationale for continual monitoring of current *and* potential competitors.

Case Study

As mentioned throughout this chapter, the key goal of competitor analysis is to understand how competitors might react to your company's actions and how you can influence competitor behavior to your company's advantage. Objectives and assumptions are what drive a competitor, and strategy and capabilities are what a competitor is doing or is capable of doing. How can you really understand competitor behavior? Think of competitor analysis (refer to Figure 4.1) as having four distinct boxes:

Box 1 = Future strategies/goals/philosophies

Box 2 = Current strategies

Box 3 = Current capabilities and resources

Box 4 = Management assumptions

The analysis occurs with the comparison of information (Step 3) in Boxes 1, 2, and 3.

A company with managers who understand their competitive environment and have a clearly thought-out growth strategy will find that Boxes 1, 2, and 3 match and are cohesive. This suggests that management's assumptions (Box 4) are minimal and that the company is a formidable competitor.

If Boxes 1, 2, and 3 do not match, you must understand what assumptions are driving management—that is, Box 4. By understanding management's assumptions, you can understand the drivers of this competitor's behavior.

This can best be explained by the following example.

Chinese Mobile Market

A competitor analysis was undertaken of a player in the Chinese mobile phone market. Briefly the following sample information was identified:

Future Strategies/ Goals/Philosophies (Box 1)	Current Strategies (Box 2)
To be the number one global player in mobile phones.	To offer the lowest price mobile phones.

Management Assumptions (Box 4)	Current Capabilities and Resources (Box 3)
That the Chinese government would continue to provide additional funding as required.	The company had substantial financial burdens and, based on its current financial situation, would be unable to repay its debts.

The key pieces of information in Boxes 1, 2, and 3 show there is a mismatch between them—that is, how can a competitor be a global player offering the lowest price phones when they cannot repay their existing debts? Thus a key assumption is operating within the company. This assumption relates to a cultural driver that may no longer necessarily be valid, and it opens up an opportunity for another competitor to offer to buy certain parts of the company, thereby reducing its debt and reliance on the government for additional funding.

While this example provides a brief overview of this technique, when collecting information for Boxes 1, 2, and 3, it is important that you cover the breadth and depth of each facet, as explained by the following scenarios:

- **Future strategies/goals/philosophies.** A competitor that is focused on reaching short-term financial goals might not be willing to spend much money in response to a competitive attack. Rather, it might favor focusing on the products it can defend. On the other hand, a company that has no short-term profitability objectives might be willing to participate in destructive price competition in which neither company earns a profit.

Competitors' goals commonly include financial issues, growth rate, market share, and technology leadership. Goals may be associated with each hierarchical level of strategy—corporate, business unit, and functional level.

The competitor's organizational structure provides clues as to which functions are deemed to be the more important. For example, functions that report directly to the CEO are likely to be given priority over those that report to a senior vice president.

Other aspects of the competitor that serve as indicators of its objectives include risk tolerance, management incentives, backgrounds of the executives, composition of the board of directors, legal or contractual restrictions, and any additional corporate-level goals that may influence the competing business unit.

Whether the competitor is meeting its objectives provides an indication of how likely it is to change its strategy.

- **Current strategies.** The two main indicators about a competitor's strategy are what it says and what it does. What a competitor is saying about its strategy is revealed in

  - Annual shareholder reports
  - Financial reports
  - Interviews with analysts
  - Statements by managers
  - Press releases

  However, the stated strategy often differs from what a competitor actually is doing, which will be evident in where its cash flow is directed, such as in the following actions:

  - Hiring activity
  - R & D projects
  - Capital investments
  - Marketing campaigns
  - Strategic partnerships and/or alliances
  - Mergers and acquisitions

- **Current capabilities and resources.** Knowledge of a competitor's objectives and current strategy is useful in understanding how it might *want* to respond to a competitive attack. However, its resources and capabilities will determine its *ability* to respond effectively.

  A competitor's capabilities can be analyzed according to its strengths and weaknesses in various functional areas. Analysis can be taken further to evaluate a competitor's ability to increase its capabilities in certain areas. A financial analysis can also be performed to reveal a company's sustainable growth rate.

  Because the competitive environment is dynamic, you need to know about the competitor's ability to react swiftly to change. Factors that slow a company down include low cash reserves, large investments in fixed assets, and an organizational structure that hinders quick action.

- **Management's assumptions.** The assumptions that a competitor's management holds about their company and their industry will help to define their moves. For example, if a player in the industry has introduced a new type of product that failed, other industry players may assume that there is no market for the product. Such assumptions are not always accurate and, if incorrect, may present opportunities. For example, new entrants might have the opportunity to introduce a product similar to a previously unsuccessful one without retaliation because incumbent companies may not take their threat seriously. Honda was able to enter the U.S. motorcycle market with a small motorcycle because U.S. manufacturers, based on their past experience, assumed that there was no market for small motorcycles.

A competitor's assumptions may be based on a number of factors, including any of the following:

- Beliefs about its competitive position and other competitors
- Past experience with a product or service
- Regional factors
- Industry trends
- Corporate cultural history

The outcome of competitor analysis is the development of a response profile of possible moves that might be made by a competitor. This profile includes both potential offensive and defensive moves. The ultimate objective of competitor analysis is an improved ability to predict competitors' behavior—and even to influence that behavior to a company's advantage.

5

Financial Ratio and Statement Analysis

Description and Purpose

A company's published annual report and accounts usually contain a bewildering array of figures, which are often difficult to analyze. *Financial statement analysis* provides managers with an understanding of a company's financial performance, competitive situation, and future prospects. It also gives insight into the company's financial decision making and its operating performance. *Ratio analysis* provides insights into the relationships between two or more amounts in a company's financial statements.

Basic Concepts Underlying Financial Ratio and Statement Analysis (FRSA)

The basic equation that expresses the relationship of assets and claims on assets is called the *accounting equation*:

Assets = Liabilities + Owners' Equity

Assets are generally classified into three categories:

- **Current assets.** Cash and other assets expected to be converted into cash within one year, such as marketable securities, accounts receivable, notes receivable, inventories, and prepaid expenses.

- **Fixed assets.** Business assets that have relatively long lives and are used in the production or sale of goods and services, such as equipment, machinery, furniture and fixtures, land, and plants.
- **Noncurrent assets.** Investments in securities and intangible assets such as patents, franchise costs, and copyrights.

Liabilities are generally classified into two categories:

- **Current liabilities.** The amounts owed to creditors that are due within one year.
- **Long-term liabilities.** Claims of creditors that do not come due within one year, such as bonded indebtedness, long-term bank loans, and mortgages.

Owners' equity is the claims of owners against the business. This is the residual amount computed by subtracting liabilities from assets. Its balance is increased by any profit and reduced by any losses incurred by the business.

Components of Financial Statements

Statements commonly used by analysts include the income statement, balance sheet, statement of changes in financial position, and statement of changes in owners' equity.

- **The income statement** summarizes the results of a company's operations in terms of revenue and expenses for a period of time called the *accounting period*. Net income is derived from the accrual measurement of revenue and expenses. The income statement is generally perceived as the most important financial statement because it reveals whether the shareholders' interests in the organization have increased or decreased for the period after adjusting for dividends or other transactions with owners. The income statement also helps users to assess the amount, timing, and uncertainty of future cash flows.
- **The balance sheet** shows what a company owns (assets) and claims against the company (liabilities and owners' equity) on a

particular date. It provides a snapshot of a company's financial
health at a particular point in time.

- **The position statement** (also known as the statement of
changes in financial position) helps to explain how a company
acquired and spent its money.
- **The statement of changes in owners' equity** shows the gap
between the amount of owners' equity at the beginning and end
of a period.

Applying ratio analysis to financial statements enables you to
make judgments about the competitive success, failure, and evolution
of a company over time and to evaluate how it is performing compared
with similar companies in the same industry. It can assist a company
in gaining an awareness of competitors' strengths and weaknesses. For
example, if you find weaknesses in a competitor's performance, then
your company may be able to take measures to exploit them.

Assessing the Appropriateness of Ratios

There are three principal benchmarks to assess the appropriateness of ratios.

The first benchmark is *the company's performance history*. It is
useful to review the ratios in the current year relative to what they
were in several prior years. This enables you to discover favorable or
unfavorable trends that are developing over time, as well as identify
any numbers that have changed dramatically in a defined period of
time.

The second benchmark is *to compare a company to specific competitors*. If the competitors are publicly listed companies, obtain
copies of their annual reports and compare each of the focal company's ratios with each of the competitor's. This is particularly helpful
in identifying why the focal company is doing better or worse than specific competitors.

The third benchmark is *an industry-wide comparison*. You need to obtain data regarding industry averages, many of which can be accessed from Internet and government sources. Dun & Bradstreet and Robert Morris Associates are two examples of commercial sources that collect financial data, compute ratios by industry, and publish the results. The information is often broken down by size of company and in a way that allows you to determine how far away from the norm any company is.

Strengths

FRSA is a helpful information overload tool. It can find patterns in large amounts of disconnected data through

- Transforming financial data into manageable and meaningful outputs
- Connecting the dynamic income statement with the static balance sheet into one integrated analysis

FRSA is versatile and easily amenable to internal company analysis and competitive analysis of rivals and industry structure. It allows you to determine a company's ability to succeed through its application of a generic strategy, such as low-cost producer, niche pursuer, or differentiator. By combining the FRSA with numerous other techniques, such as those described in other chapters contained in this book, you can gain a good picture of a company's likelihood of strategic and competitive success.

Weaknesses

Financial ratios are based on historical accrual accounting information. As such, they do not offer the analyst any direct insights into cash flow, an important component of value-based management. This can be even more important with embryonic, entrepreneurial companies that have larger burn rates and cash needs during their earlier years.

Additionally a single ratio will not give you enough information to make a judgment about a company. Additional data is necessary to make these judgments.

Accountants do not include as assets certain items that are critical to the growth and well-being of a company in balance sheets, such as the quality of its employees. Financial statements virtually ignore these increasingly important intangible assets—a key source of competitive advantage in an information or knowledge-driven economy. FRSA is inherently limited as an analytical tool for companies with valuable brand names or corporate reputations, intellectually skilled workforces, or other intellectual capital.

Not all financial statements are of equal quality. Reporting authorities and accounting overseers in separate countries may require different conventions, which can make comparisons difficult. Audited statements provide you with a higher probability of accurate financial information. However, published ratios are generally not subject to public audits, with the exception of the Earnings per Share (EPS) ratio.

Over-reliance on industry norms is akin to benchmarking for mediocrity instead of best practice. Even though it is important to use industry norms to evaluate financial performance against industry peers, caution should be applied in interpreting the results. Analysts who overly rely on industry comparisons risk leading their companies to the netherworld of what Michael Porter aptly describes as being 'stuck in the middle' of the industry's parabolic profit curve. To see how this can occur, consider an industry in which half of the rivals are pursuing a low-cost strategy while the other half are pursuing a differentiated strategy. Comparing a company's ratios to the industry norms will, by definition, target average performance. Success in meeting these average targets will necessarily relegate the company to the lowest point on the industry profit curve. At one end, the average company's cost structure will be higher than that of the low-cost specialists; at the other end, premium companies will surpass the average company's level of differentiation.

When using industry norms, you must also remain aware of comparing dissimilar industry groups—direct financial comparisons to rivals outside an industry group may only provide low short-term utility. Even comparisons within industry groups are fraught with difficulty when rival companies are operating on a different portion of the industry profit curve by virtue of their chosen low cost, differentiation, or focus strategies. Additionally, because most industry norms are calculated from aggregated financial statements, rating a company's financial performance to a diversified company will cause a critical comparability problem if the lines of business are radically different.

Making internal comparisons to past company performance is also risky. One of several manifestations of this risk is complacency from seemingly adequate improvements while in reality the company is slipping relative to the performance of rivals. This problem is especially prevalent in fast growth markets where differences in relative competitive performance may not be painful in the short term but will nonetheless have serious repercussions on long-term competitive positioning.

You should also carefully consider the effects of management choices on the results of operations as reported in the financial statements. In closely held businesses, it is not uncommon for the financial statements to reflect discretionary choices of the business owner or senior management. Sometimes significant adjustments can be required to restate the financial statements to accurately portray the operations of the business.

The choice of accounting method may have a significant impact on the income reported in the income statement and the value of the asset reported in the balance sheet. This is especially pertinent when doing international competitor comparisons and when competitors have multinational operations that potentially utilize different accounting schemes. Other technical considerations that could distort the validity of the comparison include differences in accounting policies (different depreciation schedules, inventory valuation, and capitalization), account classification, or year-ends across companies.

Even when a company's financial ratios appear to conform to industry averages, this does not mean that the company has no financial or other strategic management problems. For example, the company may be neglecting to exploit a clear differentiation advantage through which it could outstrip average industry performance. Alternatively, perhaps the company's finances look good at the moment, but a serious competitive threat could reverse them in the near future.

In short, financial ratio analysis is a useful tool for analyzing the decisions of management as they are manifest in the marketplace, but it cannot replace the insights afforded by the application of a variety of analysis tools.

How to Do It

Performing an FSRA can be divided into several steps:

- First, you must choose the appropriate ratios to analyze.
- Second, the appropriate sources must be located to provide the raw data in which to calculate the ratios—this is a topic better covered by books on the larger competitive intelligence data collection process.
- Third, you calculate the ratios and make comparisons of the ratios.
- Fourth, a check is performed for opportunities and problems.

Following are some common ratios for analyzing financial statements. Table 5.1 compiles the necessary formulas to use.

Activity or Efficiency Ratios

These include inventory, accounts receivable, and fixed and total asset turnover ratios.

Inventory

Depending on the nature of the business (retail, wholesale, service, or manufacturing), the efficiency of inventory management may have a significant impact on cash flow and, ultimately, its success or failure.

- **Average Inventory Investment Period**

  Average Inventory Investment Period = Current Inventory Balance/Average Daily Costs of Goods Sold (COGS)

  This measures the amount of time it takes to convert a dollar of cash outflow used to purchase inventory to a dollar of sales or accounts receivable from the sale of the inventory.

  The average investment period for inventory is much like the average collection period for accounts receivable. A longer average inventory investment period requires a higher investment in inventory. A higher investment in inventory means less cash is available for other cash outflows, such as paying bills.

- **Inventory to Sales Ratio**

  Inventory to Sales Ratio = Inventory/Sales for the Month

  This looks at the company's investment in inventory in relation to its monthly sales. It helps identify recent increases in inventory and is a quick and easy way to look at recent changes in inventory levels because it uses monthly sales and inventory information.

  This ratio will help predict early cash flow problems related to a business's inventory.

  However, where the only information available is based on inventory information from the previous year, it can be used to provide a rough guide.

- *Turnover Analysis*

  Inventory Turnover = Sales/Inventory of Finished Goods

  This is the most basic tool for assessing the organization's investment in inventory. It helps you to decide if the company's investment in an inventory item or groups of items is excessive, too low or just right. From a cash flow perspective, performing turnover analysis is particularly useful for finding inventory items that are overstocked.

Accounts Receivable

Accounts receivable represent sales for which payment has not yet been collected. If the business normally extends credit to its customers, the payment of accounts receivable is likely to be its single most important source of cash inflows.

The following analysis tools can be used to help determine the effect the company's accounts receivable are having on its cash flow.

- *Average Collection Period*

  Average Collection Period = Current Accounts
  Receivable Balance/Average Daily Sales
  (Average Daily Sales = Annual Sales/360)

  This measures the length of time it takes to convert average sales into cash. This measurement defines the relationship between accounts receivable and cash flow. A longer average collection period requires a higher investment in accounts receivable. A higher investment in accounts receivable means less cash is available to cover cash outflow.

- *Accounts Receivable to Sales*

  Accounts Receivable to Sales Ratio = Accounts
  Receivable/Sales

  This looks at the company's investment in accounts receivable in relation to sales. It helps you to identify recent increases in accounts receivable and can serve as a quick and easy way to examine any recent changes. The more recent information of the accounts receivable to sales ratio will quickly point out cash flow problems related to the business's accounts receivable.

- *Accounts Receivable Turnover*

  Accounts Receivable Turnover = Accounts Receivable/Average Daily Sales

  This is a measure of the average length of time it takes a company to collect the sales made on credit.

Asset Turnover

This is the ratio of sales (on the income statement) to the value of the company's assets (on its balance sheet):

Asset Turnover = Revenue/Assets

It indicates how well a business is using its assets to generate sales. Generally, the higher the ratio the better because a high ratio indicates the business has less money tied up in assets for each dollar of sales revenue. A declining ratio may indicate that it has over-invested in plant, equipment, or other fixed assets. Companies with low profit margins tend to have high asset turnover; those with high profit margins have lower asset turnover—this indicates pricing strategy. In computing this ratio, it may be helpful to compute total assets by averaging the total assets at the beginning and end of the accounting period.

This ratio indicates how well a company is using all of its business assets to generate revenue, rather than just its inventories or fixed assets. A high asset turnover ratio means a higher return on assets, which can compensate for a low profit margin.

Leverage or Solvency Analysis Ratios

Commonly used solvency ratios are debt to equity, debt to assets, coverage of fixed costs, and interest coverage.

This group of ratios is designed to help you assess the degree of financial risk that a business faces. Financial risk, in this context, means the extent to which the company has debt obligations that must be met, regardless of its cash flow. By looking at these ratios, the analyst can decide whether the company's level of debt is appropriate or not.

- ## *Debt to Equity*

  Debt to Equity = Total Debt/Total Shareholders' Equity

  This indicates the degree of financial leverage that the company is using to enhance its return. It provides a measure of the funds provided by creditors versus the funds provided by owners.

  A rising debt to equity ratio may signal that further increases in debt caused by purchases of inventory or fixed assets should be curtailed.

  Improving this ratio involves either paying off debt or increasing the amount of earnings retained in the business until after the balance sheet date.

- ## *Debt to Assets*

  Debt to Assets = Total Debt/Total Assets

  This compares the percentage of assets financed by creditors to the percentage financed by the business owners. Historically, a debt to asset ratio of no more than 50 percent has been considered prudent. A higher ratio indicates a possible overuse of leverage, and it may indicate potential problems in meeting the debt payments.

  Improving this ratio means taking steps either to increase the value of the company's assets or to pay off debt. If it goes the route of paying off debt, it will also improve its current ratio and debt to equity ratio.

- ## *Fixed Charge Coverage*

  $$\text{Fixed Charge Coverage} = \frac{\text{Profits Before Taxes and Interest} + \text{Lease Obligations}}{\text{Total Interest Charges} + \text{Lease Obligations}}$$

  This shows the company's ability to meet its fixed obligations of all types—the higher the number, the better.

  Obviously, a company's inability to meet any fixed obligation is a threat to its well-being. Many working capital loan agreements will specify that a company must maintain this ratio at a specified level so that the lender has some assurance that the company will continue to be able to make its payments.

- *Interest Coverage*

Interest Coverage Ratio = Operating Income/Interest Expense

This is also known as the Times Interest Earned Ratio. It is similar to the Times Fixed Charges Earned Ratio but focuses more narrowly on the interest portion of the company's debt payments.

By comparing the ratio of operating income to interest expense, you can measure how many times the company's interest obligations are covered by earnings from its operations. The higher the ratio, the bigger the company's cushion and the more able it is to meet interest payments. If this ratio declines over time, it's an indication that the company's financial risk is increasing.

Liquidity Analysis Ratios

These ratios indicate the ease of turning assets into cash. They include the current ratio and quick ratio. Liquidity ratios are sometimes called working capital ratios (the difference between current assets and current liabilities). Generally, the higher they are, the better, especially if the company is relying to any significant extent on creditor money to finance its assets.

- *Current Ratio*

Current Ratio = Total Current Assets/Total Current Liabilities

This is one of the most popular measures of financial strength. It is a good indicator of a company's ability to pay its short-term obligations.

The main question this ratio addresses is: "Does the company have enough current assets to meet the payment schedule of its current debts with a margin of safety for possible losses in current assets, such as inventory shrinkage or collectable accounts?" The higher the ratio, the more liquidity the company has. A generally acceptable rule of thumb for a current ratio is 2:1. But whether a specific ratio is satisfactory depends on the nature of the business and the characteristics of its current assets and liabilities. The minimum acceptable current ratio is 1:1, but that relationship is usually suggestive of potential risks or problems.

- ***Quick Ratio***

$$\text{Quick Ratio} = \frac{\text{Cash} + \text{Government Securities} + \text{Receivables–Inventory}}{\text{Total Current Liabilities}}$$

This is also known as the acid test ratio and is one of the best measures of liquidity. It describes how quickly a company can turn its current assets into cash.

The quick ratio is a more exacting measure than the current ratio. By excluding inventories, it concentrates on highly liquid assets with values that are fairly certain. It helps answer the question: "If all sales revenues stop, could the business meet its current obligations with the readily convertible 'quick' funds on hand?"

An acid test of 1:1 is considered satisfactory unless the majority of a company's "quick assets" are in accounts receivable, and the pattern of accounts receivable collection lags behind the schedule for paying current liabilities.

- ***Working Capital***

Working Capital = Current Assets − Current Liabilities

This is the amount of liquid assets a company has to build its business, fund its growth, and produce shareholder value.

The best way to look at current assets and current liabilities is to combine them into "working capital." Working capital can be positive or negative. If a company has ample positive working capital, it has the cash on hand to pay for the items it needs. If it has negative working capital, its current liabilities are greater than its current assets, and it has less ability to pay for the items it needs. A competitor with positive working capital will always outperform a company with negative working capital.

Profitability Analysis Ratios

These ratios are probably the most important indicators of a business's financial success—they demonstrate the performance and growth potential of the business. The most common of these include Return on Assets, Return on Equity, Profit Margin (which can be in either gross or net form), and Asset Turnover.

- ### Return on Assets

  Return on Assets (ROA) = Net Income/Total Assets

  This is the ratio of net income to total assets. It is a measure of how well a business is using its assets to produce more income. It can be viewed as a combination of two other ratios: net profit margin (ratio of net income to sales) and asset turnover (ratio of sales to total assets). A high return on assets can be attributed to a high profit margin, a rapid turnover of assets, or a combination of both.

- ### Return on Investment (ROI)/Return on Equity

  Return on Equity (ROE) = Net Income/Total Shareholders' Equity

  This is the ratio of net income (from the income statement) to net worth or shareholders' equity (from the balance sheet). It shows what the company earned on its investment in the business during the accounting period. This ratio compares a business's return on equity to what it might have earned on the stock market during the same accounting period. Over time, a business should be generating at least the same return that it could earn in more passive investments, such as government bonds. A high return on equity may be a result of a high return on assets, extensive use of debt financing, or a combination of the two.

  In analyzing both ROE and ROA, don't forget to consider the effects of inflation on the book value of the assets. While financial statements show all assets at their book value (original cost minus depreciation), the replacement value of many older assets may be substantially higher. A business with older assets would generally show higher return percentages than a business with newer assets.

- ## *Gross Profit Margin*

Gross Profit Margin = Gross Profits/Sales

This is the amount of sales dollars remaining after the COGS has been deducted. If a company's gross profit margin is declining over time, it may mean that its inventory management needs to be improved, or that its selling prices are not rising as fast as the costs of the goods it sells. If the company is a manufacturer, it could mean that its costs of production are rising faster than its prices, and adjustments on either side (or both) may be necessary.

The net profit margin shows the company's bottom line: how much of each sales dollar is ultimately available for the owners to draw out of the business or to receive as dividends. This ratio takes into account all of the company's expenses, including income taxes and interest.

You should have some idea of the prospective range of the company's profit margin, which will in large part be determined from historical data. If a company fails to meet its targets, it could mean that it has set unrealistic goals or is not managing as efficiently and effectively as it could. However, the ratio itself will not point to *what* a company might be doing wrong—looking at the gross margin or operating margin is a better way to address that problem.

The absolute level of profit may provide an indication of the size of the business, but on its own it says very little about company performance. To evaluate the level of profit, profit must be compared and related to other aspects of the business. Profit must also be compared with the amount of capital invested in the business and to sales revenue.

Profitability ratios will inevitably reflect the business environment of the time, so the business, political, and economic climate must also be considered when looking at the trend of profitability for one company over time. Comparisons with other businesses in the same industry can give an indication of how well management is performing compared to other companies in the same business environment.

Other Analysis Ratios—Capital Market or Shareholder Returns

The use of capital market or shareholder returns analysis ratios is probably more important for investors than it is for strategic or competitive analysis. These are more commonly thought of as investment measures as opposed to performance measures.

- ### Earnings per Share

$$\text{Earnings per Share (EPS)} = \frac{\text{Net Income–Dividends on Preferred Stock}}{\text{Average Outstanding Shares}}$$

This indicates the profitability of a company. Company earnings are income from sales or investment after paying expenses. The way in which a business conducts its operations is important when evaluating a company's earnings. Companies that are devoting significant resources to creating a new product may have relatively low earnings, but that can change when sales of the new product grow and profits rise. Meanwhile, companies that have strong earnings but are not investing adequate funds into the business may have significant problems in the future.

- ### Price/Earnings Ratio

Price/Earnings (P/E) Ratio = Current Market Value per Share/EPS

This is often referred to as "the Multiple." The earnings per share figure is usually from the last four quarters (the trailing P/E ratio), but sometimes it is from the estimates of the earnings expected in the next four quarters (the projected P/E Ratio) or from the sum of the last two quarters and the estimates of the next two quarters.

For the most part, a high P/E means high projected earnings in the future. A P/E ratio on its own doesn't give much information, however it is useful to compare the P/E ratios of other companies in the same industry to the market in general or against the company's own historical P/E ratios.

TABLE 5.1 Financial Ratios

Activity or Efficiency Ratios

Average Inventory Investment Period

Average Inventory Investment Period = Current Inventory Balance/Average Daily COGS

(The average daily cost of goods sold (COGS) is computed by dividing your annual COGS by 365 days.)

Inventory to Sales

Inventory to Sales Ratio = Inventory/Sales for the Month

Turnover Analysis

Inventory Turnover = Sales/Inventory of Finished Goods

Accounts Receivable Ratios

Average Collection Period

Average Collection Period = Current Accounts Receivable Balance/Average Daily Sales

(Average Daily Sales = Annual Sales/365)

Accounts Receivable to Sales

Accounts Receivable to Sales Ratio = Accounts Receivable/Sales

Accounts Receivable Turnover

Accounts Receivable Turnover = Accounts Receivable/Average Daily Sales

Asset Turnover

Asset Turnover = Revenue/Assets

Leverage or Solvency Analysis Ratios

Debt to Equity

Debt to Equity = Total Debt/Total Shareholders' Equity

Debt to Assets

Debt to Assets = Total Debt/Total Assets

Fixed Charge Coverage

$$\text{Fixed Charge Coverage} = \frac{\text{Profits Before Taxes and Interest + Lease Obligations}}{\text{Total Interest Charges + Lease Obligations}}$$

Interest Coverage

Interest Coverage Ratio = Operating Income/Interest Expense

Liquidity Analysis Ratios

Current Ratio

Current Ratio = Total Current Assets/Total Current Liabilities

Quick Ratio

$$\text{Quick Ratio} = \frac{\text{Cash + Government Securities + Receivables–Inventory}}{\text{Total Current Liabilities}}$$

TABLE 5.1   Financial Ratios

Liquidity Analysis Ratios

Working Capital
Working Capital = Current Assets − Current Liabilities

Profitability Analysis Ratios

Return on Assets
Return on Assets (ROA) = Net Income/Total Assets

Return on Investment (ROI)/Return on Equity
Return on Equity (ROE) = Net Income/Total Shareholders' Equity

Gross Profit Margin
Gross Profit Margin = Gross Profits/Sales

Other Analysis Ratios—Capital Market or Shareholder Returns

Earnings per Share

$$\text{Earnings per Share (EPS)} = \frac{\text{Net Income−Dividends on Preferred Stock}}{\text{Average Outstanding Shares}}$$

Price/Earnings Ratio
Price/Earnings (P/E) Ratio = Current Market Value per Share/EPS

Methods of Ratio or Measure Comparison

No single ratio has a meaning by itself, but comparing ratios is critical for effective financial ratio analysis. A helpful solution to combat analytical myopia is to strike a balance between the industry norm, historical analysis/internal benchmarking and competitive external benchmarking approaches.

There are two basic ways of using financial ratios. The first way is to compare the company's ratios with those of other companies in the industry. The second way is to compare the company's present ratios with its own past performance ratios.

Industrial Comparison

In industrial comparison we look at the company's performance in relationship to its competitors to show any differences in their operating efficiency. Once the problem is found, the company can take action to correct it. These industry averages can be found in publications like Dun & Bradstreet's Key Business Ratios.

There are several ways of obtaining financial ratios or comparisons for industries and companies, some of which are free and others that are available for a fee, as described in Table 5.2:

TABLE 5.2   Information Sources for Industrial Comparisons

Resource	Free/For fee
Yahoo! Finance provides company profiles from Capital IQ, which provides users with information on over 9000 public companies, including contact information, business summaries, officer and employee information, sector and industry classifications, business and earnings announcement summaries, and financial statistics and ratios. Yahoo adds stock charts based on historical data from Commodity Systems, Inc. (CSI) and links to other resources. **Available from: http://biz.yahoo.com/i/**	Free
The Wall Street Journal offers ratios from its website. The Valuations And Ratios page offers access to significant data needed to assess a stock's worth and a company's value. Statistics compare data on a quarterly, fiscal year, and trailing 12-month basis. In addition to the most recent figures, P/E numbers are available for the last five-year period. Quarterly and year-end figures are from 10-Q and 10-K SEC filings respectively. **Available from: http://online.wsj.com/**	Free
File 101 DISCLOSURE DATABASE® provides business and financial information on approximately 12,000 public companies. This information is derived from reports filed with the U.S. Securities and Exchange Commission (SEC). Financial information includes annual and quarterly balance sheets, income and cash flow statements (in a structured as reported format), annual financial ratios, and weekly price-earnings information. **Available from www.dialog.com**	For a fee

TABLE 5.2   Information Sources for Industrial Comparisons

Resource	Free/For fee
File 519 D&B—Duns Financial Records Plus® (DFR) provides up to three years of comprehensive financial statements for over 2.9 million private and public companies. Depending on the company, information provided may include balance sheet, income statement, and 14 of the most widely used business ratios for measuring solvency, efficiency, and profitability. **Available from www.dialog.com**	For a fee
Key Business Ratios on the Web is an online analysis tool that provides immediate access to competitive benchmarking data that is updated twice a year. You can obtain industry benchmarks compiled from D&B's database of public and private companies, choosing from 14 key business ratios (choose a one-year or three-year set of ratios) for over 800 lines of business. **Available from http://www.dnb.com/us/dbproducts/sales_marketing/research_verify/key_business/**	For a fee
Almanac of Business and Industrial Financial Ratios is the first step in helping to determine a company's true measure of performance and value. The comprehensive resource puts 50 comparative performance indicators at the practitioner's command and covers all of North America (U.S., Canada, and Mexico) using NAICS data. The Almanac provides financial information that is calculated and derived from the latest available IRS data on nearly 5 million U.S. and international companies. The Almanac gives you accurate performance data for 50 operating and financial factors in 199 industries. **Available from www.amazon.com**	For a fee

TABLE 5.2 Information Sources for Industrial Comparisons

Resource	Free/For fee
Annual Statement Studies: Industry Default Probabilities and Cash Flow Measures, 2005–2006 is the original Annual Statement Studies® and is the only source of financial ratio benchmarks derived directly from more than 190,000 statements of financial institution borrowers and prospects. These financial statements go directly to RMA from member institutions that get their data straight from the businesses they serve. Originally produced by Robert Morris Associates, these are now available from the Risk Management Association. **Available from: http://www.rmahq.org/RMA/**	For a fee
QFR: Quarterly Financial Report for Manufacturing, Mining and Trade Corporations is also accessible online at the U.S. Census Bureau. It presents estimated statements of income and retained earnings, balance sheets, and related financial and operating ratios for corporations with at least $5 million in assets. **Available from: http://www.census.gov/csd/qfr/**	For free
The Value Line Investment Survey is a comprehensive source of information and advice on approximately 1700 stocks, more than 90 industries, the stock market and the economy. **Available from: www.valueline.com**	For a fee

TABLE 5.2   Information Sources for Industrial Comparisons

Resource	Free/For fee
Standard & Poor's Industry Surveys are the fastest way to come up to speed on the players and events impacting over 50 of the largest North American and global industries.	For a fee
Each report is authored by a Standard & Poor's industry research analyst and includes the following sections: Current Environment, Industry Trends, How the Industry Operates, Key Industry Ratios and Statistics, How to Analyze a Company, Glossary of Industry Terms, Additional Industry Information References, and Comparative Company Financial Analysis.	
Available from: clientsupport@standardandpoors.com or http://sandp.ecnext.com/coms2/page_industry	
Worldscope Fundamentals is an extensive source of financial data including Financial Ratios (annual and five-year averages) including growth rates, profitability, leverage, liquidity, asset utilization, foreign business statistics, loan losses and deposits (for banks), earning assets (for insurance companies), and footnotes to financial ratios.	For a fee
Available from Thomson Financial (formerly Datastream) at www.thomson.com	
Integra Information focuses on private companies in the U.S. and collects information from government sources (including the IRS) and many other sources—32 different data sources. The Integra Infobase represents the financial performance of over 4.5 million privately held businesses operating in over 900 industries.	For a fee
Available from www.integrainfo.com	

Trade associations and individual companies often compute ratios for their industries and make them available to analysts. Published financial statements on the Internet also offer a source of raw material for companies not covered by these sources.

To deal with corporations of significantly different sizes in a particular industry, it can be helpful to create "common-size financial statements." The common size is usually 100. This procedure can help you to identify when a competitor departs from industry norms. It will allow you to ask a more refined set of questions in order to gain an understanding of the causes driving this phenomenon.

Across Time Performance

You can also spot problems by comparing a company's present performance to how well it did in the past few years. This will give an indication of how well they are progressing in correcting any problems. By looking at the past trend, a company can determine how effective it is in accomplishing its goals. You should use the same time frame in making any comparison. If you don't, effects caused by recessions or seasonal fluctuations could result in erroneous conclusions or judgments.

Consolidation and Segmented Analysis

Financial statements of public companies are legally mandated to provide segmented reporting in addition to consolidated operations. Most countries require public companies to provide enough information to explain about three quarters of the company's revenue. However, due to the competitive sensitivity of segmented information, public companies generally follow the letter of the law rather than the spirit of the law; that is, proprietary concerns outweigh the need for public accessibility to information. Therefore, segmented reporting only includes the bare minimum of information regarding the revenue, net income, and total assets of each segment. The only supplement to this meager reporting is information about the industry and geographic dispersion of its facilities and customers.

Although segmented reporting is certainly more valuable than consolidated information when comparing a company to its distinctly diversified rivals, it should not be relied upon. The accuracy and comparability will be minimal because segmented revenue will be derived from internal transfer prices, and the basis for allocating costs will be unknown to the external analyst.

Despite the requirement to reconcile or integrate the segment information back into the consolidated statements, segmented data will not provide enough information to calculate many ratios. Further, even when ratios can be calculated, you must remain aware of these limitations when performing ratio analysis on segmented data.

Remember that a company's financial statements are only a starting point for analysis. If a statement shows that accounts receivable have experienced a significant downward trend over the last few years, it could mean that the company is collecting the accounts more aggressively (which is good), or it could possibly mean that it is writing off accounts as uncollectible too soon (which is bad). Individual numbers aren't good or bad in themselves. You may have to dig behind any numbers for the reason. The key is to use FRSA to spot trends and anomalies, and then follow these up with further investigation.

To complete the picture, you must acquire more information about the company's products, people, technology, and other resources that may give it a competitive advantage in the marketplace. One of the best sources of supplemental information is the non-financial section of the annual report. This section often provides an outline of top management's views on the company's future and ability to compete.

FRSA is a critical part of a larger, integrated financial statement analysis plan. This plan should include the following key steps:

1. Determine the objectives of the financial statement analysis.

2. Review the current and predicted economic conditions in the industry in which the company operates.

3. Consult the annual report and other regulatory filings to glean information about management and the company's accounting methods.

4. Analyze the financial statements using the means described in this chapter.

5. Draw relevant conclusions based on the initial objectives.

Case Study

Dell Inc. in 2005

In seeking to assess Dell's financial performance during the 1998–2004 period, the company's financial statements needed to be assessed. Financial ratios indicate the following:

- Dell's revenue grew at a compound annual rate of 22.4% from fiscal 1998 to fiscal 2004.

- Earnings rose from $944 million in fiscal 1998 to $2645 million in fiscal 2004—a compound average growth rate (CAGR) of 18.7%.

- Diluted earnings per share rose from $0.32 in 1998 to $1.01 per share in fiscal 2004—a CAGR of 21.1%.

- The company earned 42.1% return on shareholders' equity in fiscal 2004 versus 43.5% in fiscal 2003, 26.5% in fiscal 2002, 38.7% in 2001, 31.3% in 2000, 62.9% in 1999, and 73.0% in 1998.

- The number of outstanding shares was trending downward.

- Profit margins were good and have improved since 2002 but were still not as high as the 1998–1999 period:

	2004	2003	2002	2001	2000	1999	1998
Gross profit margin	18.2%	17.9%	17.7%	20.8%	20.7%	22.5%	22.1%
Operating profit margin	8.6	8.0	5.7	8.4	9.0	11.2	10.7
Net profit margin	6.4	6.0	4.0	6.8	6.6	8.0	7.7

- Fiscal 2002 was not a good year for Dell.
- Operating expenses as a percentage of sales revenue were trending downward—a clear sign of improving efficiency:

1998	1999	2000	2001	2002	2003	2004
11.4%	11.3%	11.7%	11.9%	11.7%	9.9%	9.7%

- The company's R&D spending increased from $204 million in 1998 to $464 million in fiscal 2004—but was down from 1.65% of revenues in 1998 to 1.11% in 2004 (a sign of growing R&D efficiency or a weaker management commitment to R&D or a lesser need for Dell to perform R&D?).
- The company's operations were generating positive cash flows—$3.5 billion in fiscal 2003 and $3.7 billion in fiscal 2004.
- The company was in a strong cash position, with $11.9 billion in cash and marketable securities as of January 30, 2004.
- The company had little long-term debt—$505 million in 2004 versus shareholders' equity of $6.3 billion, a very good debt-to-equity ratio.

As a result of financial ratio and statement analysis, it is fair to say that Dell's financial performance has been reasonably impressive (aside from fiscal 2002) and that the company is in good overall financial shape—declining expense percentages, low long-term debt, $11.9 billion in cash and short-term investments, and improving profit margins since the lows of 2002.

Data for case study adapted from two sources: A.A. and J.E. Gamble, "Dell Inc. in 2005: A Winning Strategy?" Case Study 7, *Thompson*; A.J Strickland, *Strategy: Winning in the Marketplace, 2ⁿᵈ Edition* (New York: McGraw-Hill/Irwin, 2006).

6 —————————————————————

Five Forces Industry Analysis

Description and Purpose

The Five Forces Industry Analysis, developed by Michael Porter,[1] is designed to give you an understanding of an industry and its participants. The purpose of industry analysis is to analyze the economic and market forces that will ultimately influence an industry's profit potential. Identifying the profit potential or "attractiveness" of an industry provides the foundation for bridging the gap between your firm's external environment and its internal resources.

Porter classifies the five forces or "rules of industry competition" as follows:

1. Threat of new entrants
2. Bargaining power of suppliers
3. Bargaining power of buyers
4. Threat of substitute products or services
5. Degree of rivalry among existing competitors

The objective of this analysis is to

- Identify the profit potential of an industry
- Identify the forces that would harm your company's profitability in that industry

- Protect and extend your competitive advantage
- Anticipate changes in industry structure

A proper understanding of the five forces is important in developing your company's competitive strategy. The ultimate aim of the analysis is in developing competitive actions to cope with and, ideally, influence or change these forces in favor of your firm.

The scope of each of the five forces is covered in the following sections.

Threat of New Entrants

Everything else being equal, industries that are very easy for new organizations to enter are more difficult to compete in than ones with higher barriers. The nature of entry barriers affects the level of difficulty facing companies wishing to enter an industry. If entry barriers are low, new entrants will increase the demand and prices for inputs, resulting in lower industry profitability. New entrants ordinarily face several entry barriers. These include things such as

- **Entry-deterring price.** The cost of entry exceeds forecasted revenue—often, existing players will lower their prices to thwart a competitive entry.
- **Incumbent retaliation.** Existing companies often have substantial resources and the willpower to fight new entrants.
- **High entry costs.** Often, substantial portions of the start-up costs are unrecoverable.
- **Experience effects.** Existing companies' accumulated experience in the industry often translates into lower cost structures.
- **Other cost advantages.** Access to valuable inputs and suppliers, proprietary technology, or the best locations may already be controlled by existing companies.
- **Product differentiation.** The high cost of marketing new brands may pose significant entry barriers not faced by existing companies that have well-known brands, customer loyalty, and the flexibility to co-brand other products.

- **Distribution access.** This also includes the need to pay incentives to distributors to persuade them to carry new products.
- **Government.** Public bodies can provide subsidies for existing companies, enforce compliance with regulations, or develop policies that restrict entry.
- **Switching costs.** It can be expensive or inconvenient for customers to switch to a new product.

Bargaining Power of Suppliers

Suppliers may have the ability to influence the cost, availability, and quality of input resources to companies in the industry. When considering this force, suppliers must be thought of more broadly than just those providing raw material inputs. This group can also include those groups governing or providing labor (unions or professional bodies, for example), locations (landing slots at airports), or channels (the broadcasting spectrum), among other things.

Suppliers' bargaining power may be influenced by the following:

- **Concentration.** Supplier bargaining power will be high where an industry is dominated by fewer players than the industry it sells to unless substitute inputs are available.
- **Diversification.** The proportion of total sales that a supplier has with a particular industry will vary inversely with supplier power. For example if a supplier's revenue is totally sourced from one industry, its power over the industry will be lower than a supplier that only sells 20 percent of their total goods to an industry.
- **Switching costs.** Supplier bargaining power will be weaker if companies in an industry can switch suppliers easily or inexpensively.
- **Organization.** Supplier organizations such as cartels or unions or the presence of patents or copyright will increase supplier power, and thus their collective bargaining power.
- **Government.** In many economies, the government can function as a supplier, whether of land, rights to compete, licenses, and so on and can therefore exert substantial bargaining power.

Bargaining Power of Buyers

Buyers can influence industry structure and force prices down by such actions as comparison shopping or by raising quality expectations.

Buyers' bargaining power may be influenced by the following:

- **Differentiation.** Products with unique attributes will decrease buyers' power. Commodity products that are difficult to distinguish will increase their power.
- **Concentration.** Where there are few buyers and they represent a high proportion of a company's sales (for example, a government body that serves as the primary buyer of pharmaceuticals for citizens living within its boundary), buyer power will be high.
- **Profitability.** Buyers with low margins, lesser resources, and/or profits will be more price-sensitive.
- **Quality.** Where quality is important, buyers may be less price-sensitive.

Threat of Substitute Products or Services

Not only does an organization have to worry about competition from companies within the industry seeking to provide similar products or services to a group of customers, it also needs to concern itself with companies from outside the existing industry who seek to provide alternatives not provided by companies in the existing industry. Industry competitors would always prefer the threat of substitute products or services to be low. Market displacement by existing or potential substitutes can be influenced by the following:

- **Relative price/performance trade-off.** The risk of substitutes is high where existing products or services offer favorable attributes at low cost.

- **Switching costs.** The threat of substitution is low where switching costs—from one product or service that customers are currently using—are high.
- **Profitability.** A reliable substitute product that is profitable may displace or disrupt existing products.

The Degree of Rivalry Among Existing Players

Of all the five forces, rivalry among existing players is nearly always the most important in determining the attractiveness and potential profitability of an industry. All else equal, existing companies in an industry prefer to face lesser competitive intensity and rivalry. Strangely enough, and for a variety of sometimes counter-intuitive reasons, some degree of rivalry and a small number of competitors are typically superior to no rivalry or what is otherwise known as a monopoly situation. The intensity of competition within an industry is determined by the following:

- **Market growth.** When strong, market growth in the existing industry reduces rivalry and thereby the probability of retaliation.
- **Cost structure.** When fixed costs are high, over-capacity occurs during demand troughs, and the fight for market share by existing rivals intensifies.
- **Barriers to exit.** For low-profit companies, barriers to exit include asset specialization, fixed costs of exit, emotional attachment, or the product's market importance in a company's overall strategic intentions. The higher these are, the more intense the rivalry will be in an industry.
- **Product switching.** Product differentiation may protect the company from unwanted switching to other competitors by existing customers.
- **Diversity.** Where an industry has many companies of equal size and competitive position, rivalry will be more intense. Entry from difference sources, such as the Web, will also increase rivalry.

Strengths

Five Forces analysis will help you to identify the main sources of competition and their respective strengths and to build a strong market position based on competitive advantage.

This technique, in fact, provides the raw analytical framework necessary to develop a strategy that will help insulate your company from competitive forces and provide it with competitive advantage. Additionally, it is a good technique for understanding industry evolution, as it will allow you to identify windows of opportunity to capitalize on changes in any of the five forces.

Central to this technique, particularly when trying to understand how an industry will evolve, is the identification that a change in one force will affect the other forces, which may result in the alteration of an industry's structure and its boundaries. This analysis can then

- Forecast future changes in each of the five competitive forces
- Discover how these changes will affect the other forces
- Discover how the interrelated changes will affect the future profitability of the industry
- Discover the strength of your company's position in this evolved industry
- Discover how you might change the strategy to exploit the changing industry structure

The Five Forces model will also assist you with long-range planning, as it will focus your attention on the mutual dependency between the industry forces that change over time and the fact that a business strategy should both reactively defend against *and* actively manage these forces.

Weaknesses

The main weakness, according to critics of the Five Forces model, is that it underestimates the core competencies or capabilities that may serve as a company's competitive advantage in the long term. Industry structure is one factor that determines a company's profitability; others like unique organizational resources will be important as well. The model is designed to analyze individual business unit strategies within unique industries. It does not take into account the synergies and interdependencies within a corporation's overall portfolio.

Strict interpretations of the model do not fully recognize the importance of social and political factors within or impacting on each of the five forces. For example, the role and influence of government as an industry stakeholder, which some argue should be treated as a separate sixth force, can directly impinge on the competitive parameters of the industry.

Porter himself has acknowledged that the Five Forces model is primarily concerned with what makes some industries, and some positions within them, more attractive—but it does not directly address *why* or *how* some companies are able to get into advantageous positions in the first place and why some are able to sustain these positions over time while others are not.

The implicit advice the Five Forces model delivers for formulating strategy may direct a company to focus on industry-level characteristics, encouraging it to allocate resources on influencing the industry's structure even though it may not uniquely benefit from the changes, but may also allow competitors to benefit from them. This course of action may be justifiable if industry structure is the dominant determinant of company performance.

How to Do It

Applying the Five Forces model involves three major steps and several substeps, described in the following sections.

Step 1: Collect Information

The first step involves specifically identifying your industry. This is not always easy to do and can require you to try several means, including looking at existing demand and supply patterns around specific products and services, using pre-existing classification sources like the North American industrial classification system (NAICS, formerly known as the standard industrial classification or SIC), or gaining agreement from business experts familiar with your competitive context. Once the industry is identified, you will need to collect information to identify the characteristics of each of the five forces (see Figure 6.1) and then examine and assess their impact on the industry.

While much of the information required in this step can be obtained from published sources, it is important to use human sources where possible to improve the objectivity of your analysis and to identify possible market intentions. This process requires identifying the main sources of competitive pressures, which are

- Rivalry among competitors
- Threat of substitute products
- Threat of potential entry
- Bargaining power of suppliers
- Bargaining power of buyers

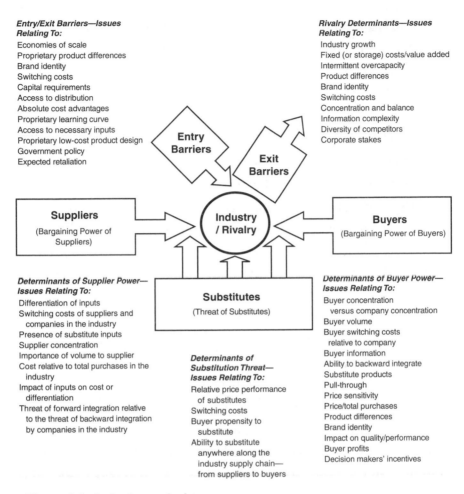

Entry/Exit Barriers—Issues Relating To:
Economies of scale
Proprietary product differences
Brand identity
Switching costs
Capital requirements
Access to distribution
Absolute cost advantages
Proprietary learning curve
Access to necessary inputs
Proprietary low-cost product design
Government policy
Expected retaliation

Rivalry Determinants—Issues Relating To:
Industry growth
Fixed (or storage) costs/value added
Intermittent overcapacity
Product differences
Brand identity
Switching costs
Concentration and balance
Information complexity
Diversity of competitors
Corporate stakes

Entry Barriers

Exit Barriers

Suppliers
(Bargaining Power of Suppliers)

Industry / Rivalry

Buyers
(Bargaining Power of Buyers)

Substitutes
(Threat of Substitutes)

Determinants of Supplier Power— Issues Relating To:
Differentiation of inputs
Switching costs of suppliers and companies in the industry
Presence of substitute inputs
Supplier concentration
Importance of volume to supplier
Cost relative to total purchases in the industry
Impact of inputs on cost or differentiation
Threat of forward integration relative to the threat of backward integration by companies in the industry

Determinants of Substitution Threat— Issues Relating To:
Relative price performance of substitutes
Switching costs
Buyer propensity to substitute
Ability to substitute anywhere along the industry supply chain— from suppliers to buyers

Determinants of Buyer Power— Issues Relating To:
Buyer concentration versus company concentration
Buyer volume
Buyer switching costs relative to company
Buyer information
Ability to backward integrate
Substitute products
Pull-through
Price sensitivity
Price/total purchases
Product differences
Brand identity
Impact on quality/performance
Buyer profits
Decision makers' incentives

Figure 6.1   Industry analysis

Adapted from Michael E. Porter, *Competitive Advantage: Creating and Sustaining Superior Performance* (London: Collier Macmillan Publishers, 1985).

Step 2: Assess and Evaluate

The second step involves assessing and evaluating the five forces in light of your organization's and other rivals' competitive ability. This includes determining the direction of the force (that is the arrow) around the industry and the relative strength of each force by giving each of them a value, indicating if it is strong, moderate, or weak. One way to do this is to use a scale of 1 to 5, with 1 indicating a weak force and 5 indicating a strong force (see the case studies at the end of this chapter). An important input into this process is providing a logical explanation of how each competitive force works and its role in the overall competitive picture.

For example, the competitive environment is unattractive and profitability will be harder to achieve when rivalry is strong, competition from substitutes is strong, entry barriers are low, and suppliers and buyers have considerable bargaining power.

The competitive environment is attractive and profits more easily generated when rivalry is low to moderate, there are no good substitutes, entry barriers are relatively high, and suppliers and buyers have poor bargaining power. The returns earned by rivals in these attractive industries should be greater over a designated span of years than those earned by rivals in unattractive ones.

A company whose strategy and market position demonstrates a good understanding of these five forces can earn above average profits, even when some or all of the five forces are strong.

The ultimate goal of most business or competitive analysis is to identify the ability of your company to successfully compete within its industry, given the collective strength of the five forces. A comparison of your company's resource strength with regard to the size of the "fit" gap with each of these five forces will provide valuable insight on strategic opportunities and threats.

Step 3: Develop Strategy

The third step requires repeating the first two steps in light of industry change and evolution. To improve the usefulness of this analysis, long-term industry trends should be analyzed to determine whether the profitability of the industry is sustainable and how this will affect your company's competitive position. Trends include, among other things, proposed government legislation and regulations, social and consumer trends, international changes and trends, guiding economic forces, and technological trends.

Now, integrate these long-term trends within the broader context of corporate strategy to find the tightest "fit" between your company's resources, capabilities, and the external environment. This involves three types of strategic scenarios: reactive strategy against likely competitor moves; proactive strategy to manipulate changing forces already in motion; and proactive strategy to explicitly force change in one or all of the five forces.

Industry structure fundamentally affects strategic choices. Understanding how an industry will evolve provides important direction for selecting and managing strategy around these five criteria. Each competitive force should be constantly monitored for its impact on your overall company strategy and the opportunities it represents for extending competitive advantage. The interactions amongst these forces and trends must also be kept in consideration.

Finally, not all industries are alike—for companies with product portfolios across numerous industries, this technique should be repeated for each industry.

Case Study

Applying the Five Forces Model to the U.S. Passenger Airline Travel Industry

(5 = strongest, 1 = weakest)

Threat of entry—weighting 4

- Deregulation in the 1980s reduced legislative barriers.
- High capital intensity, offset to a lesser degree by the ability to lease aircraft and hire ground crews on contract
- Limited availability of terminal slots offset to some degree by use of secondary or less-accessible airports.

Threat of substitutes—weighting 3

- Improved information and communication technologies lessen the need for some forms of physical air travel.

- Market growth of profitable business class is slowing due to the impact of information technology reducing the need for face-to-face communication.

Bargaining power of buyers—weighting 4

- Hyper-competition has made air travel more closely resemble a commodity, resulting in overcapacity.

- Price sensitivity of consumers has not been significantly offset by loyalty programs.

- Greater availability of real-time price and other travel factor considerations through presence of air travel sites via the World Wide Web.

- Sale of tickets directly by existing rivals' websites lessens the need to share rent with travel agents.

Bargaining power of suppliers—weighting 4

- Increasingly militant unions (flight attendants, machinists, pilots, for example) have eroded economic rent associated with producer surplus.

- There are very few suppliers of aircraft for certain forms (trans-oceanic) of long-distance travel.

- Public entities have been less likely to provide public funding for airport expansion, new landing slots, or larger/more runways.

- Bankruptcy regulations allow existing competitors to favorably restructure existing contracts and lessen the financial burdens created by some suppliers.

Degree of competitive rivalry—weighting 4–5

- Market share warfare is the industry norm.

- Some long-standing carriers, particularly the full-service, long-haul-oriented ones, have folded or gone into bankruptcy.

- Competition frequently devolves to considerations of pricing.

- Growth in travel class offset by larger planes and competitive entry, resulting in overcapacity and lower margins.

- High proportion of fixed costs and resulting variable cost pricing through heavy discounting to maximize contribution margin from excess capacity.

- High exit barriers for larger, more heavily invested carriers.

Conclusion: All the competitive forces are at least moderately strong and in some cases very strong. The attractiveness of the airline industry is low, and it will generally be difficult to sustain attractive levels of profitability in light of the current set of forces. Having stated that, some airlines have managed to create strategies that effectively offset many of the negative forces and achieve reasonable levels of profitability, reinforcing the need we previously described to develop effective strategies in light of the forces and trends impacting them.

Case Study

Applying the Five Forces to the Global Pharmaceutical Drug Industry

(5 = strongest, 1 = weakest)

Threat of entry—weighting 3

- High capital requirements (average drug requires $200 million in R&D) and substantial unrecoverable marketing expenditures.

- Hence, niche strategies are the only feasible basis of competition for new entrants that, if successful, are frequently subject to aggressive takeover overtures.

- High degree of specialized expertise required to successfully participate over the long run.

- Patent protection promotes and protects innovation.

Threat of substitutes—weighting 2

- Few substitutes exist for drug therapy, and it is often much cheaper than hands-on medical and surgical interventions.
- Generic products only available after lengthy period of patent protection disappears.
- Other forms of therapy remain less trusted and typically more risky from a scientific sense than pharmaceuticals

Bargaining power of buyers—weighting 1–2

- Doctors, not patients, usually make the purchase decision based on product attributes and efficacy, not price.
- When consumers do make the purchase decision, they show a high brand loyalty that works against private-label drugs.
- Some organized buying groups (health maintenance organizations, public bodies such as provincial health care providers, and so on, for example) have, to a degree, eroded the discretionary powers of pharmaceutical manufacturers.

Bargaining power of suppliers—weighting 2

- Many of the raw inputs to pharmaceuticals are commodities.
- Biotechnology and gene therapy are still in the developmental stage.
- Many of the promising new biotech companies have or will be acquired by established drug companies.
- Highly specialized human resources can be difficult to acquire in some pharmaceutical therapy areas.

Degree of competitive rivalry—weighting 3

- Continual product innovation by rivals creates new or growing demand.
- Aging baby boomers and growing life spans will foster growth.
- A high percentage of unrecoverable costs such as R&D and marketing/distribution increase barriers to exit.
- Offsetting the effect of high premiums offered by incumbents for acquisitions of smaller companies.

Conclusion: All of the competitive forces now facing this industry are fairly weak to moderate. The attractiveness of the industry remains good, and profitability of rivals in the drug industry is relatively high. The analyst must be careful to consider existing and potential trends that may impact the forces and their interactions, a task that may show that future attractiveness and profitability may be relatively harder for pharmaceutical companies to achieve in future years.

Endnote

1 See Michael Porter, Competitive Strategy: Techniques for Analyzing Industries and Competitors (London: Collier Macmillan Publishers, 1980).

7

Issue Analysis

Description and Purpose

Issue analysis aids the strategic and competitive intelligence (CI) efforts of companies by helping them anticipate changes in their external environments and to become more proactive in shaping it through their influence on public policy (PP). It is also a useful technique for a company to use to position itself to deal with changes in public policy. The opinions of stakeholders can affect corporate decisions related to consumer protection, environmental protection, financing options, health and safety, marketing, operating standards, product packaging and placement, and site location, among others.

Public environmental intelligence provides early warning of threats and opportunities emerging from the global PP environment that can affect a company in achieving its strategy. Public environment intelligence can be used in a variety of decision-making areas, including

- **Creating, changing, or defeating legislation or regulation.** For example, enabling Sunday retail sales, modification of tariff regimes, and compliance scheduling timetables.
- **Changing operating standards to adapt to evolving PP.** Companies such as YouTube can broadcast clips of cable or network shows using new web-enabled technologies.

- **Altering employee performance procedures or labor practices to adapt to PP issues.** For example, providing benefits to same-sex couples, not using underage contract employees in less developed countries, and providing equal opportunity to employment or advancement regardless of one's demographics.

- **Changing the company's mission or taking a leadership role in PP issues.** For example, chemical companies' responsible care initiatives in voluntarily phasing out controversial practices ahead of legal standards.

- **Taking a public communication stance on key policy issues.** For example, several large Internet companies vocally addressing privacy and free speech issues.

- **Changing vendors/suppliers as a result of PP.** U.S. retailer Wal-Mart establishing a preference policy of purchasing from local suppliers in countries where it has retail stores, when it could be done competitively.

- **Entering or exiting product or service lines to adapt to PP issues and standards of liability or public expectations.** For example, Internet service providers refusing to host "hate" or terrorist-oriented sites, former defense-related companies moving into commercial areas connected to their former contracts, and the sale of products being banned in one country to countries where the bans are not similarly legislated.

Issue analysis is also part of the larger (strategic) issue management process. The strategic purpose of issue analysis is to assist decision makers in identifying, monitoring, and selecting issues for action that may impact the company's profitability and competitiveness. It helps strategic decision makers to avoid surprises that emerge from change in the broad environmental STEEP factors and to better address STEEP issues, regardless of whether they are opportunities or threats (see Chapter 10, "Macroenvironmental (STEEP/PEST) Analysis," for more on STEEP analysis).

There are several key lessons you need to note when utilizing issue analysis:

- The time over which an issue develops can vary enormously; sometimes it can develop in days or weeks, sometimes in years or even over decades.
- Many issues will get transformed as they evolve—there are many twists and turns among issues and stakeholders in the PP-making process that can shift the expected trajectory of an issue. This makes planning and the consideration of different scenarios (see Chapter 9, "Scenario Analysis") paramount.
- There is uncertainty surrounding which issues will actually make it onto the PP arena. Some issues are best resolved through proactive measures, while selected others can be safely ignored in the decision making process.

Strengths

Conducting issue analysis can enhance a company's competitiveness through improved strategic decision making based around proper researching PP and STEEP factors. It gives management the advantage of selecting the highest impact issues that the organization should respond to, as opposed to being distracted by lower impact issues and needlessly wasting valuable resources.

Issue analysis also helps in the early identification of emerging issues, thus providing lead time to coordinate internal organizational and external environmental responses. It can reduce the risk and uncertainty of adapting organizational initiatives in a changing environment. It promotes the management of issues rather than reactions to them.

The active monitoring and addressing of issues helps the company to deflect concerns before they become major problems and to transform emerging trends into corporate opportunities. It provides an organization-wide process for anticipating and dealing with STEEP factors, enabling the company to be in tune with societal expectations and to avoid serious public mistakes that could harm its credibility and reputation with critical stakeholders.

Weaknesses

Although issue analysis can be beneficial to organizations in several ways, its applicability and usefulness is constrained by several factors. The most common of these include

- It is a helpful tool for organizations facing PP challenges, but it might not always assist them in achieving a competitive or strategic advantage. This is because some issues are institutional by nature and must be dealt with by the entire industry or the largest competitors, thereby not providing the kinds of differential advantages companies often seek in making resource allocations.

- It must be carried out on an ongoing basis. For this to happen, inputs must be generated by regular monitoring and scanning of the company's environment. This is difficult for most companies not only due to the overwhelming amount of data available in the environment but also because of the difficulties of selecting the important data.

- Many issues defy logical or rigorous assessment because they contain emotional or attitudinal factors, often due to media attention, which make their evolution difficult to predict.

- There are few yardsticks with which to evaluate the effectiveness or success of the issue analysis process. This can lead to the under-allocation of resources, even though many managers recognize that it is important regardless of the unreliability of results.

- It is difficult to see direct correlation between intervening in issues and resultant financial or market measures.

How to Do It

The task in issue analysis is to take the environmental data gathered during scanning and monitoring and to sort it into informational categories, rank it, evaluate it according to selected criteria, and draw conclusions for managerial decisions. Experts suggest that three tasks are precursors to effective issue analysis:

- Issue identification and forecasting
- Issue assessment
- Selection of issues and response

Step 1: Issue Identification and Forecasting

Before an issue can be analyzed, it has to be identified. The techniques listed here are some of the more popular ones for identifying issues.

- **Content analysis.** This technique involves scanning newspapers, web logs, journals, books, articles, reports, newsletters, speeches, and so forth. The approach and the results can be either quantitative or qualitative.
- **Scenario development.** Scenarios are written descriptions of plausible alternative futures based on specified assumptions about relevant environmental forces (frequently categorized as STEEP) and their interactions. We describe this in greater depth in Chapter 9.
- **Survey techniques.** The major techniques in this category include public and stakeholder opinion polling, attitudinal surveys, and Delphi panels. Delphi panels use a sequence of questionnaires distributed to experts in which the responses to one questionnaire are used to produce successive questionnaires. Any set of information available to some experts and not to others is passed along, allowing each person on the panel to have the same information to produce his or her forecast. Delphi panels improve the use of expert opinion through polling based on anonymity, statistical display, and feedback of reasoning.

The actual issue analysis process then consists of three components:

- Forecasting
- Assessment
- Selection of issues to allow the organization's decision makers to determine the nature of potential responses

The first step is to anticipate or forecast the development of the issue that your organization monitors. There are several tools that can assist you with this:

Four-Stage Life Cycle Progression of PP Issues

One particularly helpful tool for forecasting the sequence and development of issues is known as the *issue life cycle*. It is based on the premise that issues tend to evolve through a fairly logical progression from when they first appear on the company's radar screen until they are no longer prevalent in the company's environment.

Two caveats should be noted in using the issue life cycle:

- Issues can be derailed at almost any stage of the life cycle by other matters, as other issues grow in attention, as political or social attention shifts, as media coverage of them declines, or when interest groups and stakeholders take effective actions that either accelerate or impede progress.
- The amount of time between issue stages can vary a great deal from country to country, government to government, and issue to issue.

As issues evolve, public attention increases until a peak point is reached, while managerial discretion steadily decreases. Following are the four common stages through which PP issues progress.

1. **Formation.** Issue development usually signals structural changes and gives rise to the recognition of an issue. It is often difficult to identify the subtle, often imperceptible, changes that occur in

societal expectations at this stage. Often, the observations of certain stakeholders (academics, authors, government sponsored researchers, media commentators, public crusaders, PP researchers, think tanks, or web commentators) can be helpful in identifying expectation shifts. It is usually best for a company to attempt to influence the evolution of an issue at this early stage, when it is easier to set the boundaries and terms of the debate.

2. **Politicization.** This stage sees the creation of a special set of stakeholders known as *interest groups*, who want to see the issues resolved. They frequently try to get the issue placed on the PP agenda for consideration by public bodies. Specific remedies will start to emerge during debate. A company has less control over shaping the issue at this stage but can still have an influence if it is willing to take an active role.

3. **Legislative formalization.** This is the stage at which the issue has peak public attention. It is defined in more concrete terms (operational and legal) and frequently results in new legislation or regulations being introduced. This is usually the last chance the company has to influence the development of an issue, and any changes at this stage are usually costly, require heavy lobbying, grassroots activity, and public communications.

4. **Regulation/litigation.** At this stage, public attention plateaus, enforcement procedures become routine, and penalties apply to those who violate the law. It is now even more difficult and costly for a company to effect change in the issue.

Figure 7.1 provides a view of the issue life cycle and shows how the four-stage model evolves. It also shows the nature of the discretion available to the organization as it determines when it will respond to the issue, depending on where it is in the cycle.

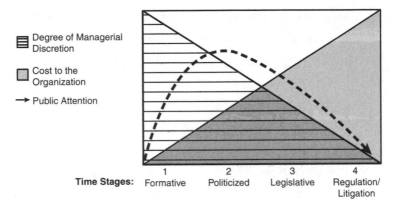

Strategic Dimensions of Public Issues

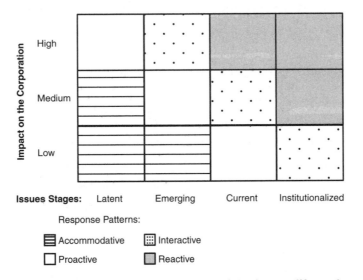

Figure 7.1   Decision-oriented applications of the issues life cycle model

Adapted from R. A. Bucholz, *Business Environment and Public Policy: Implications for Management, 5th Edition* (Upper Saddle River, NJ: Pearson Education, Inc., 1995).

Seven-Stage Progression of PP

The four-stage model just described is not the only one you can use to understand the evolution of issues. You can also identify the development of issues through the following seven stages:

1. **The problem.** The public feels general dissatisfaction over events in the STEEP environment, although they may not yet have reached consensus as to what the problem is.

2. **The label.** This is where a stakeholder, usually an interest group, addresses the issue and is able to attach a label to it.

3. **Crystallization.** The media gets wind of the issue and promotes it in the public arena. The reason for the problem is now clear.

4. **Solutions.** Numerous solutions to the problem emerge as the media continues to fan the issue. An affected company should be involved in shaping the agenda by now, as it will have little opportunity to realistically do so later.

5. **Legislation.** Political leaders get involved in the issue. They propose laws to address it. It now goes in the directions called for by public officials.

6. **Implementation.** The newly-passed laws are implemented by government agencies or departments. Legal action through the courts may take place if stakeholder groups perceive that the implementation is not in the spirit of the legislation.

7. **New problems arise.** New issues often grow out of the solutions to older ones. This can often start the cycle over again. Over- and under-regulation are examples of where issues get recycled.

Issue Expansion Map Approach

Then there is the issue expansion map approach, which identifies how an issue expands and how various stakeholders get involved. It consists of four groups:

- **Identification groups.** These are the first to become involved as the dispute expands beyond original participants. They are relatively powerless unless they consolidate with other groups.
- **Attention groups.** They tend to be organized around a small set of issues important to their membership. They are easily mobilized and have resources and access to the media, giving them power to expand the issue beyond their membership.
- **Attentive public.** These are well-educated and well-read members of the public in which are found society's opinion leaders.
- **General public.** Issues expand to this group because either the organization did not contain the issue at the attention-group level and/or because the issue is relevant and symbolic to them.

Issue Timing Approach

Another useful way to classify issues is according to timing, for which there are four major categories of issues:

- **Latent issues.** These are issues that are still not widely discussed in the media or by activist groups and other stakeholders. The scanning of these issues should focus on detecting if pressure is building, which might make the issue more important in the future.
- **Emerging issues.** These are PP questions that have three underlying characteristics:
  - The issue is still evolving as are the positions of the contending parties.
  - The issue is likely to be the subject of formal government action in the next few years.
  - The issue can still be influenced by the organization.
- **Current issue.** This is being debated or otherwise acted on within governmental institutions. Specific policies to resolve the issue are being legislated and debated by elected or appointed officials.

- **Institutionalized issue.** PP has been formulated and adopted as an attempt to resolve the issue. Approved policies are being implemented, most likely within a government agency or department.

Each of the approaches identified above for Step 1 is equally valid. It is up to you as the analyst to select which one would be most appropriate for your organizational needs.

Step 2: Issue Analysis and Assessment

Some of the techniques described in Step 1 can also be used to help you assess issues, especially Delphi panels and scenario development. Several other techniques are frequently used for analyzing and assessing issues, the most popular of which are discussed in the following sections.

Issues Distance Approach

One approach is to look at issues based on the distance between the organization and the issues under consideration. Issues would then be identified into three broad categories:

- **Current issues.** These are already under consideration by PP makers (stage 3 of the issue life cycle—see Figure 7.1), and organizations are forced to react to them.
- **Emerging issues.** These are still forming (moving from stage 1 to stage 2 of the issue life cycle) and are likely to be coming onto the formal PP-making agenda in the form of legislation in the near future. The company can still influence these issues by proactive and pre-emptive public affairs actions.
- **Societal issues.** These are vague and frequently remote concerns that may or may not affect business interests in the future. For the time being, and until they become better understood, they are not issues with which the company should be actively concerned.

Issue Impact Approach

Another approach is to base the classification of the identified issue on the number of people affected, the *severity* and *immediacy* of impact of the issue, and the *cost* of solving the problems relating to the issue. The use of these three criteria results in the following classification:

- **Universal issues.** These issues affect a large number of people, have a direct and personal impact on them, and are viewed as being serious. They are usually not of a permanent nature and are characterized by such events as energy and inflationary crises or a regional uprising by small groups. In these cases, the public generally looks to government for a quick solution.

- **Advocacy issues.** These are issues for which the public seeks governmental action to resolve. They are usually complex and build steadily over time. Issues such as the deregulation or regulation of certain industries, the provision of child daycare facilities, or foreign investment guidelines commonly fit into this category.

- **Selective issues.** These issues typically concern specific stakeholder groups. They usually generate costs to the public, but the benefits tend to go to the stakeholder groups who promoted the issue. The stakeholders tend to be identifiable by characteristics such as demography (for example, the unique job and retirement concerns held by baby boomers), geography (for example, urban dwellers concerned about the provision of satisfactory schools in run-down downtown areas), occupation (for example, the provision of benefits to migrant laborers), or sector (for example, the protection of certain forests from logging activity).

- **Technical issues.** These issues are generally not well known nor a concern to most members of the public. Experts or specialists are most concerned about these issues, and they usually end up being settled within the regulatory framework.

Issues Priority, Leveraging, and Scoring Matrices

Given the large number of issues in an organization's environment, you need to make an assessment of all the issues in order to recommend to decision makers which ones should be selected for action and resource allocation. Because all organizations have limited resources, efforts should be made to determine where the organization's actions produce the greatest net-positive effects.

To guide you through this process, there are several important questions that you need to answer:

- Where is the issue in its stage of development?
- How probable is it that the issue will evolve so that a government body will legislate on it and cause the issue to have a material impact on the organization?
- What is the likely effect of the expected PP on the organization's profitability?
- Does the organization have the capabilities to influence the issue evolution process or the range or nature of possible governmental responses?

Answering these questions requires taking the list of issues generated within the identification phase and placing them in the cells of a matrix bounded by the selection of two variables. Among the variables most frequently used are *probability* (the likelihood that the issue will occur) and *impact* (the severity of the possible effect of the issue). These are often combined into a 3x3 matrix, with the variables ranging from high to medium to low, resulting in nine cells, each of which suggests a different priority for subsequent action on behalf of the company. Common versions of this matrix are presented in Figure 7.2.

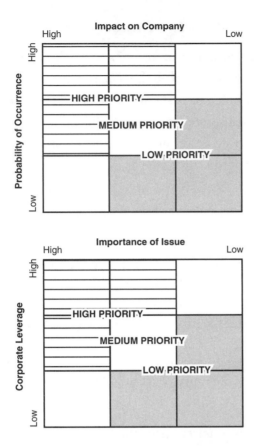

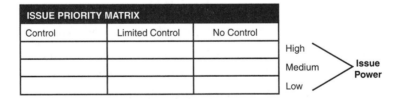

Figure 7.2   Issues priority, leveraging, and scoring matrices

Adapted from: A.B. Gollner, *Social Change and Corporate Strategy: The Expanding Role of Public Affairs* (Stamford, CT: Issue Action Publications, 1983); E Sopow, *The Critical Issues Audit, The Issue Management Workbook Collection* (Leesburg, VA: Issues Action Publications, 1994).

Step 3: Selection of Issues—Response Patterns and Types

A company's response to an issue needs to be a coordinated and planned set of actions, some of which may be internal and some of which will occur in the external or PP environment. It is helpful to consider these response patterns in making an action recommendation to the organization's decision makers. There are several ways that an issue may be responded to by an organization, including the following:

- The organization could alter its behavior, that is, its policies or activities, in such a way as to reduce or eliminate the pressures stakeholders are feeling. Johnson & Johnson did this with the packaging and sealing of its pain medication, Tylenol, after it was discovered that it had been tampered with. One side benefit of proactive behavior such as this was that the company may have forestalled regulation requiring it to take costlier or possibly less effective steps.

- The organization might try to bring its stakeholders' expectations of corporate behavior and performance closer to its own perceptions of its behavior and performance.

- The organization could enhance its stakeholder communication and educational efforts about its activities and policies in the public arena. This is frequently done today using web-based technologies and communication channels.

- The organization may contest the issue in the public opinion arena. This could be done through lobbying government decision makers, using the court system and legal challenges, applying grassroots pressure to the issue, or through advocacy advertisements and editorials.

- The organization could ignore the issue and hope it goes away or that time might resolve the matter in its favor.

Table 7.1 presents a political issues alternative matrix. It suggests that there are two dimensions to consider when planning a response to an issue. The first dimension is whether a direct or indirect mode of attack should be launched, while the second dimension looks at whether the focal unit of analysis should be an issue for the organization.

TABLE 7.1   Political Issues Alternatives Matrix

Mode of Attack	Orientation Issue	Group
Direct	Defuse the Issue	Attack the Group
Indirect	Blur the Issue	Undermine the Group

Adapted from Mahon (1989).

Four different tactics arise from these two dimensions as follows:

- **Defuse the issue.** This is a symbolic action that lacks real substance; for example, it might require the organization to set up a special committee to look into the issue, fire the leader, or say it will change its action/policy amid publicity with no intention of doing so.

- **Blur the issue.** Bring in other stakeholders, add issues, refine the current issue, postpone action while awaiting more research, or discuss all the reasons (constraints) why it cannot comply or respond.

- **Attack the group.** This is a riskier tactic where an organization raises questions about the legitimacy of an individual or group in an attempt to discredit them.

- **Undermine the group.** Co-opt stakeholders, bypass the leadership by making direct appeals to members, and use secondary sources of influence.

Another alternative classification scheme for preparing responses to public issues addresses whether the organization can resist, bargain, capitulate, terminate, or cease the activity that has brought about the issue. See Table 7.2 for examples of where each of these strategies and tactics are used.

- **Total resistance.** The organization refuses to change, repulses all challenges, or forces the environment to change or adapt to its goals.

- **Bargaining.** The organization bargains or compromises so that adjustments on all sides are required.

- **Capitulation.** The organization ends the bargaining with external actors, seeks a replacement, or changes its environment, all the while seeking the best solution for itself and exoneration.

- **Termination.** The organization ends the relationship with the external group and seeks a replacement.
- **Cessation of activity.** The organization, unwilling or unable to adapt or respond to changes demanded, disbands.

TABLE 7.2 Strategies and Tactics for Political Response

Strategies	Tactics	Examples
Resistance	Persuade and propagandize	Ford and Pinto
	Deny responsibility	Nestle and Infant Formula
		Ford Explorer rollovers
	Question other stakeholders' legitimacy	Tobacco industry
	Countercharge and diversionary tactics	Discrimination against smokers
Bargaining	Positive inducements	Union Carbide and the town of Institute, West Virginia
	Negative inducements	Medical practitioners withholding their services in order to force policy changes
Capitulation	Concede; seek best solution or exoneration	J&J and Tylenol
		P&G and Rely Tampon
Termination	Cease relationships with external stakeholders	GD Searle and IUD
		Levis staying out of China
Cessation	Dissolve the organization	File bankruptcy

Adapted from Mahon (1989).

The eventual outcome of issue analysis is the determination of a handful of issues that would be most important for the organization to act upon. Although we have provided several ways of identifying, classifying, and prioritizing issues, we do not want to suggest that the process does not contain a good degree of subjectivity. This is largely due to the perceptions of uncertainty and risk that are always prevalent in the issue environment.

The issue identification, analysis, and response process rarely unfolds in the linear, sequential fashion described in this chapter.

In the chaotic STEEP environment in which organizations operate, issue analysis and management are multilayered, iterative, trial
and error processes that must continuously adapt to evolving conditions. Uncertainty is ever present. However, it is clearly possible to do
better than competitors by learning and applying some of the tools discussed in this chapter.

Case Study

Issues Priority Assessment Process at Minnegasco

Minnegasco (now part of CenterPoint Energy), an American gas
utility company operating in Minnesota, has an issue analysis
process in place. When looking at their issues, their specialists rate
the external forces that can impact the company's success with factors such as the credibility of the groups initiating the proposal, the
opposition's strengths and weaknesses, the impact on the state's
budget, the positions of the governor and relevant state agencies,
and their ability (or lack thereof) to get coalitions to work with
them.

Once the issues are rated, they then compile an average score for
each legislative initiative. That score is weighed against the degree
of financial impact to the company, the likelihood for success, and
any other public affairs impacts, including the impact the initiative
will have on their public affairs relationships. These three elements—chance for success, financial impact, and public affairs impact—are taken together and averaged.

During issue analysis, Minnegasco analysts will then ask themselves
questions such as

- Are we going to harm or improve legislative relationships with
  this effort?

- How are other utilities in the industry going to react?

- How are our customers going to react?

- What other coalition actions are we going to have to deal with?

Minnegasco case study adapted from K. Sundberg and P. Shafer, Ed., "Using the Tools of Quality to Assess State Government Relations," *Adding Value to the Public Affairs Function*, Washington, DC: Public Affairs Council 1994: 195.

Case Study

Issues Priority Rating for Xerox's Washington Office

Xerox's Washington office had developed a ranking scheme for identified PP requiring action for which a planned program could be developed with an identified completion point. The issues relate to areas of interest where Xerox wishes to maintain a degree of activity or awareness. The ranking approach is

Priority Rating

1. Issue has high potential impact on Xerox and will require a high level of Government Affairs Office activity; may be longer term; high impact potential requires priority treatment.

2. Less Xerox-specific impact but important enough to require active monitoring; adequately covered by a third-party organization, but should include Government Affairs Office involvement in third-party activity.

3. Low potential impact for Xerox or very long-term issue with little or no current activity; Government Affairs Office will attempt to monitor but will rely on third parties for active monitoring and input.

Xerox case study adapted from R. Scheerschmidt and P. Shafer, Ed. "Quality in the Washington Office," *Adding Value to the Public Affairs Function*, Washington, DC: Public Affairs Council 1994: 256.

8

Political Risk Analysis

Description and Purpose

Political risk arises from actions taken by a government or any instability caused by unexpected government decisions or events that may lead to business loss. In many industries and markets, government decisions can make or break a company's fortunes. As such, political risk analysis (PRA) is a valuable tool when considering the impact of governmental policy, politics, and public events on a company's business and its competitive position.

The definition of political risk is important in understanding the strategic rationale by which you should examine it. Too narrow a definition can result in you working with improper conceptualizations and badly directed data gathering and selection. For the purpose of this chapter, we have chosen to adopt a broad definition of political risk as any activity by a host government or appointed administrative leadership group that could contribute to business harm or loss, including wars, unrest, border disputes, tariffs, taxes, changes in party leadership or coups, and related actions. Socio-political issues such as corruption, protests, social strife, and threats to physical and intellectual assets are also major contributors to potentially risky environments.

More and more companies are choosing to outsource facets of their businesses to countries where labor is inexpensive. One form of outsourcing, *offshoring*, is the relocation of a business activity or process to another country. Many of the popular host countries for off-shoring, such as the Philippines for example, lack a stable middle-class. The possibility for disruption remains high in environments where the standard of living for the working class is low and unemployment rates are relatively high—about 40 percent of the population in the Philippines live below the poverty line, and a substantial portion of the population is illiterate.[1]

Governments with lax attitudes on intellectual property can become an issue for any company planning to manufacture in those countries.

Many countries are also dependent on a small number of major fuel exporting countries, including several that have high levels of political risk—such as Iran, Libya, Venezuela, or Yemen. Trouble in any of these countries can affect industries around the globe as demand outpaces supply in this vital resource market. Factor in interconnected markets, offshoring, the economics of the world's oil market, and ongoing turmoil in lesser developed countries, and one can see how political instability can have far-reaching effects.

Strengths

It is easy for companies to be frightened away from countries that are viewed as unstable because of the political risks associated with them. But avoiding these markets can mean missed opportunities. Where there is typically high risk, there is generally also decreased competition, greater political flexibility, cheaper rents and labor—all things these nations need to offer in order to be attractive for investment and offset the risk levels they hold. By assessing the extent of the risks and being able to weigh the risks and opportunities, a company can determine if the risks are worth the potential gains and, if so, create contingency plans to deal with them.

PRA can be conducted up to a point using open, available, and inexpensive (if not free) sources of political risk data and information, much of it available on the Internet. Many multinationals and even some technologically savvy small and medium-sized enterprises have established environmental scanning systems to automatically capture and categorize this type of information off the Web. Due to advances in communication technology (including improved translation methods) and the higher frequency of inter-country travel, gaining primary information about the political situation in other countries has become less expensive and generally easier.

Companies that institutionalize a PRA capability into their decision-making processes can save money and time when making decisions about investing or doing business in foreign countries. PRA can also enlarge a company's network of contacts and may help it to quickly and more effectively identify better partners to assist its efforts to develop promising markets for its goods or services in the new countries.

There are many good sources of political risk information that can be purchased, subscribed to, or contracted through consultancy arrangements. Although some of these products and services may appear to be expensive, the information they contain may help a business avoid mistakes or plan for contingencies for which they would otherwise be unprepared. However, you need to help decision makers avoid being "penny wise and pound foolish" when it comes to devoting the appropriate level of resources in the decision to invest in new markets, particularly less developed or undeveloped ones, where some of the best opportunities for growth and profit may exist for the future.

The positive relationship between risk and rewards—higher risk is associated with higher rewards and vice versa—means that those companies that do the process well stand to lessen the risk of their decisions and reap a higher portion of the potential rewards available in new foreign markets.

Weaknesses

PRA can be complicated and elusive. Attempts to standardize and quantify dynamic, simultaneous events and isolate them to create direct cause-and-effect relationships have not provided the most stable foundations for the process. Ultimately, political risk experts try to assign numbers to human events, actions, and concepts that are constantly developing and unfolding, which is never an easy or precise task. When it comes to the study of political risk, many companies focus on the visible results or symptoms of political problems—mostly because they are the ones that are newsworthy and therefore appear to be the most important—rather than on the root of the problems. This bias can cause individuals to overweigh or underweigh key facets of their analysis. You must remain vigilant to qualify and quantify your data and data sources before applying them to the models you are using. However, even with the elaborate techniques and sophisticated models used by many companies, the results still often are surprising.

Data collection is the foundation for the validity of political risk scoring, and it is often flawed. Models based on historical data may also be flawed because past actions are no sure indication of future behavior. This observation is more likely to be true in the political arena of activity than for other STEEP categories, such as social, economic, environmental, and technological, due to its shorter life cycles.

Political risk assessment models are often comparative, and it is difficult to procure the same data for different countries when the data is subjective. Much of the data gathered is in the form of opinions, which are highly subjective and can frequently be biased. Interviewed "insiders" (that is, residents or citizens of the country being studied) may be biased toward the country or biased against the home country of the interviewer. Given that this is the case, different studies of the same country will often deliver vastly different results. Apart from potential biases, expert interviewees may simply attach different meanings to variables or interpret questions differently, thereby introducing unintended biases.

In lesser developed countries, much of the social, economic, and demographic data may not be published. If it is published, it may not reflect the actual state of the market. Many cultures where corruption is endemic have well-developed black markets where the exchange of cash, bribes, and goods go unrecorded. You must understand the quality, reliability, and validity of your data and data sources when performing political risk analyses.

Problems with data collection, lack of objectivity, looking to past events to predict the future, and the lack of specificity are problems that regularly plague the field of PRA. Therefore, although the discipline has been practiced for centuries and has been thoroughly documented and researched in the last four decades, it has yet to develop a commonly accepted body of knowledge or become universally standardized in terms of its practice and processes.

How to Do It

Like most of the analysis techniques in this book, analyzing political risk is part art and part science—and not necessarily equal parts. The artistic side of the balance is more easily done by those who are experienced and well-versed in the vagaries of the political terrain in various parts of the world, but some of the more robust political upsets in history were not predicted by anyone, analysts included. By definition, any time someone tries to gauge risk, something unexpected can happen. The most prudent practitioners will try to play out the outcomes of several potential scenarios.

An important element in understanding the discipline of political risk is dividing it into macro- and microrisk.

Macrorisks are described as being environmental in nature, unforeseen, political in origin and motivation, and generally directed at all foreign businesses. *Microrisks* are described as being more subtle, harder to gauge from outside the country, and although generally less consequential, more common than their macro cousins. Both macro and microrisk can be further divided into societal and governmental categories:

- **Societal macrorisk** refers to the instability caused by civil wars, terrorism, coups, major shifts in society's values, unions, religious disagreements, revolutions, national work stoppages or any other politically charged civil event that is detrimental to a foreign company. A prominent, but certainly not the only, example of societal micro-political risk is the "9/11" event in the U.S.—a poignant example of societal micro-risk that originated from outside the host country. Although terrorism, like the subway bombings in the U.K., train bombings in Madrid, the discotheque bombings in Bali, and other violent acts against host countries are less common than some other political risks, the results can be catastrophic and have global impact (on the travel and tourism industry, for one).

- **Governmental macrorisk** encompasses all actions by a host government that can have negative effects on foreign businesses. Some of these actions include high interest rates and inflation, nationalization and expropriation, limits on the repatriation of assets and profits, and a dramatic change in leadership and general bureaucracy. A dramatic example of this sort of risk occurred in Cuba when Fidel Castro's newly emerged government carried out mass appropriations of foreign corporate assets. A less extreme, though far more common, example is high tariffs in countries trying to attract foreign business. India is one of these countries—with roughly one quarter of the population still living beneath the poverty line, economic growth relies on foreign investment—yet tariffs are as high as 20 percent in some areas.[2]

- **Societal microrisks** include boycotts, activism, some acts of terrorism, and competition from other multinationals. A good example of this type of risk is Chinese consumers' threats to boycott Japanese goods on more than one occasion in recent decades due to the Japanese government's failure to fully acknowledge the atrocities committed in China in the 1930s and 1940s; hence, the Chinese are sensitive to any perceived slight by the Japanese.

- **Governmental microrisks** are those that are directed toward a specific foreign country or industry. They may include selective nationalization, prejudicial tax systems, equity regulations, content and hiring rules, supporting indigenous competitors, disregarding contracts, and putting controls on pricing. For example, an August 2005 bid by the China National Offshore Oil Company (CNOOC) to acquire U.S.-based Unocal Corporation was immobilized by the U.S. Congress. The U.S. Energy Security Bill was amended to obligate the U.S. Government to get involved in any proposal by a Chinese company to take over a U.S. oil company. This brings to light another risk—souring diplomatic relations between host and foreign countries can affect business opportunities and the nature of competition in the larger marketplace. It had been speculated that the U.S. Congress reacted adversely to CNOOC's bid for Unocal because China had yet to truly open up its market to U.S. companies.

Figure 8.1 provides a summary breakdown of the micro and macrocomponents of political risk. The arrows between the boxes at the third level exemplify that changes in one area can create political risk in another. For example, a change in societal attitudes (societal microrisk) may mean that citizens put pressure on politicians to change laws. Some stakeholders might feel that international competition is destroying the local economy and agitate for increased protection. A political party pressing to stay in power will be tempted to appease their electorate and change laws (governmental macrorisk), making it harder for multinationals to compete in the host country. Alternatively, an autocratic totalitarian regime (governmental macrorisk) repressing an uneducated militant public may result in a coup (societal macrorisk), which causes business interruption and losses.

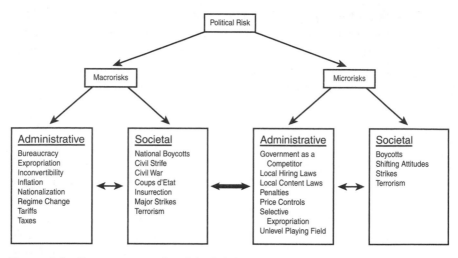

Figure 8.1   Components of political risk

Adapted from Simon, Jeffrey D., "Political Risk Assessment: Past Trends and Future Prospects." *Columbia Journal of World Business* 27 (1982): 62–71.

As should be evident by this point, the processes identified here are not sufficient to anticipate political risk, nor do they anticipate or help to plan what to do if your company is negatively affected by political factors. However, they are starting points in assessing political risk and can provide helpful insights into the likely politically derived problems a company may face with its operations in a different country. Other (nonpolitical) factors must also be considered. It is helpful to involve other functional areas of the company such as the legal department, risk management, asset management, government relations, public affairs, and communication experts, in determining the execution and implementation sequences.

Qualitative Techniques

Two of the most popular techniques for collecting qualitative information appropriate for this type of analysis include the "grand tours" and the "old hands" techniques.

Grand Tours

This technique is typically applied subsequent to conducting analysis of a foreign market. If the initial research shows a market in a country is attractive enough to warrant further consideration, the company may then be justified in sending a team to serve as inspectors. This "visit team" meets with government officials and local business people to assess the political climate and reports back to management.

The grand tours approach sounds simple enough, but it is fraught with difficulties and is by no means a replacement for comprehensive due diligence. The information received from officials and locals is often provided selectively. Designated individuals in the country being visited will allow foreigners to see what their officials want them to see and are unlikely to bring to light many of the more covert risks, such as corruption, black markets, bureaucratic inefficiencies, and other potential hindrances to profitability. Although useful as a tool, the grand tours approach should be seen as just one component or a complementary source of data in a larger PRA process and strategy.

Old Hands

Another useful component for assessing political risk involves seeking out individuals who have substantial prior or current expertise in the area, country, markets, or political system in question. Individuals hired as independent consultants with backgrounds in academia, politics, business, journalism, or a combination of these disciplines can offer useful and intuitive insights and an understanding of the history and future of political situations to a depth that simple observance or statistical models cannot often reach. Sometimes, individuals with this expertise already reside as employees within your organization!

There are always trade-offs to be considered between the flexibility and perceived objectivity of hiring experts as independent consultants versus the contextual understanding that a current employee has of the organization and its strategies. Notwithstanding these

trade-offs, the predictions gathered via these means, albeit more educated than first-time assessors of a new market, are also speculative
and may not actually happen.

Quantitative Techniques

There are five statistical techniques that can be helpful in evaluating potential political risk. Although a full examination of these techniques is beyond the scope of this chapter, it is important to know that
they are used by major companies and consultants. These five tools are

- Rank ordering
- Decision tree analysis
- Multiple regression
- Discriminant analysis
- Integrated approach

Many companies like to hire services that use a complex combination of these models to give a ranking to each country. What follows is
by no means an endorsement, but an overview of the sort of information that is available from professional companies along with the
methods they use to compile their data. Some of the more popular
ones include the BERI (Business Environmental Risk Index), PSSI
(Political System Stability Index), the DESIX (Deutschbank Eurasia
Group Stability Index), and WPRF (World Political Risks Forecast).

A practical problem with indices like these is that they do not offer much advice to help a particular company that is looking strategically at a specific situation. They were designed for purposes other
than specifically addressing a company's strategic concerns. They are
also almost fully composed from historical data and may not be overtly
or accurately predictive toward the present or the longer term.

Another helpful construct for analyzing political risk was developed by Alon and Martin.[3] They attempted to create a model, which
is future-oriented, comparative, flexible in terms of adjusting weights,

and applicable to different political circumstances and systems. Alon and Martin's framework takes into account the governmental, societal, and economic aspects of macrorisk and looks at the causes of these elements from an internal and external perspective, thereby creating a model with six components, which are adapted and summarized in Table 8.1.

TABLE 8.1   PRA Elements

	Internal	**External**
Governmental	• Degree of elite repression • Degree of elite legitimacy • Likelihood of regime change	• Likelihood of political violence • Involvement in international organizations • Regulatory restrictions
Societal	• Degree of fragmentation • Degree of congruent cleavages • Sense of alienation	• World public opinion • Disinvestment pressures • Regional diversity and incongruent interests
Economic	• Per capita GDP growth • Income distribution • Likelihood of economic goals being met	• Policies on foreign investment • Likelihood of debt problems • Likelihood of currency problems

Internal Factors

Governmental

With regard to "degree of elite repression" and "degree of elite legitimacy," the following questions are asked:

• How does the government treat its citizens?
• Does the government use force or heavy restrictions against them?

The "degree of legitimacy" aims to help you determine the degree to which citizens have faith in the governing body. The scores of the first two factors point to the likelihood of the third factor: the "likelihood of a regime change." If there is a high "degree of elite repression," and the people feel as though the regime is illegitimate, you would need to account for a higher probability that the government will be uprooted in the future. If this were the case: Who would be likely to take over? What changes would be made? What would be the new regime's feeling toward foreign investment?

Societal

When looking at the societal factors, Alon and Martin identified the "degree of fragmentation," "congruent cleavages," and the "sense of alienation" as contributors to political risk. A society is fragmented if it is very heterogeneous. Religion, social class, ethnicity, land claims, and language differences can all divide societies. It is easy to see that countries like Belgium, India, Malaysia, Rwanda, and South Africa are fragmented, but some surprisingly developed regions also show this division. For example, Canada's Anglo, French, and Aboriginal populations make it a fragmented society, and France has had recent difficulties with immigrant and minority groups being involved in violence because of their long-standing perceptions that they aren't getting appropriate recognition from the majority group that composes French society. The more diverse the society, the less likely is it that all groups will get their needs met. If some of these groups are poor, disenfranchised, and have little or no opportunity for improvement, the result can be "congruent cleavages," which can lead to political instability. Feelings of alienation from the home country, be it nationalistic or xenophobic, can also lead to conflict.

Economic

When analyzing economic factors for political risk, trends in "per capita GDP growth" is an indicator of economic growth (provided GDP growth is growing faster than the population). The "income distribution" will tell you if the middle class is developing or whether it even exists. The "likelihood of economic goals being met" looks at whether or not the government's policies are aligned closely with its stated goals.

External Factors

Governmental

Assessing a country for the "likelihood of political violence" means one has to look at the host country and surrounding territories. The repercussions from war are obvious, but tensions in nearby countries resulting from refugees or displaced warring groups can have a big impact on a host country's political stability. "Involvement in international organizations" can point to stability because membership of the International Monetary Fund or the World Bank means that the country probably doesn't have major sanctions against it, and it may also be eligible for aid in the wake of temporary instability. "Regulatory restrictions" include tariffs, restrictions on money entering and leaving the country, and trade barriers. Expropriation is included in this category as well.

Societal

"World public opinion" can be a formidable force. Up until it achieved its current democratic, non-apartheid status, South Africa (RSA) was seen as a leper by much of the world. Apartheid policies from successive RSA governments caused problems for foreign investors—not because it created a danger or just from a matter of principle—but because citizens of other countries were applying "disinvestment pressures." "Regional diversity and incongruent interests" can cause instability, such as seen in the Middle East and parts of Africa where there have been long-standing tribal or turf wars during which land and valued resources have frequently changed hands.

Economic

Treaties and alliances can help combat the potential of negative future economic "policies on foreign investment." Some of these policies can include protectionism and limits on repatriation and ownership. The "likelihood of currency problems" arises in cases of massive inflation, which leads to currency devaluation and can make the flow of imports and exports to the host country very difficult, introducing the "likelihood of debt problems."

It is important to note that Alon and Martin's model sees all symptoms of political risk as falling into at least one of these six categories. The practical implementation of the model involves four steps, outlined as follows:

1. Identify variables as outlined previously.
2. Assign each variable a score in the range of -2 to +2, with a negative correlation between height of risk and numerical score. Therefore, +2 means low risk, -2 means high risk, and 0 is neutral. Two things to keep in mind when assigning scores are first, this is a comparative tool, and scores for one country will always be judged in the context of their relation to others being studied (be that the home country or other potential sites for investment); and second, as this tool attempts to be a predictor, one should attempt to anticipate potential for future change in a positive or negative direction when assigning scores—this can be best done by looking at the political risk at two specific times and applying trend analysis processes to the future period.

3. Assign a weight to each variable, reflecting the importance that your company places on it. It is usually helpful to generate these weights by surveying executives and developing a consensus-based score.

4. Calculate the aggregate score for each country based on the variable scores and weights and compare the relative risk associated with each country.

For an example of an application of the model, see the Baser Foods case study below.

A few caveats apply to effectively employing this method. All of the external information gathered is not going to be helpful if it is not viewed in terms of how the company would handle turbulence in light of its own strategies, strengths, and weaknesses. Creating a proactive and mutually beneficial relationship with a host government can go a long way to minimizing risk over time and increasing the company's strength. Intuitively, it can be suggested that multinationals will be less exposed to microrisks if the company is willing to use the local work force, adapt to suit local conditions and address local needs, and work co-operatively with local officials.

Finally, the company must understand its own risk tolerance. For example, companies operating in the energy market must have a strong tolerance for risk and depend on elaborate contingency planning to offset risk. Pharmaceutical companies, on the other hand, have relatively less risk tolerance and choose to locate in more stable environments. Ongoing monitoring of the company's strengths, assets, liabilities, and contingency plans must take place. An integrated risk management approach can be helpful because, conceptually, integrated risk management attempts to view all uncertainties in relation to each other rather than viewing them in isolation.

Corporate reactions to unstable circumstances are often too late because people have an innate desire to minimize and deny the possibility of unfortunate events. It is beneficial to create an organizational culture in which this form of denial is discouraged, and imagining and anticipating potentially risky situations is encouraged and rewarded. Field employees can be an excellent source for precursors to change. Are the lines of communication open throughout the company—particularly for those isolated or lone employees based in foreign countries? Is the company organized so that vital information about political changes, events, risks, and trends passes through as few hands as possible to get to decision makers? Do employees know they can come to you with "What if?" situations?

If the answers to all of these things are affirmative, then good PRA will benefit the company and its decision making. If it is not, no amount of PRA will keep the company from experiencing adversity abroad.

Case Study

Baser Foods—An Illustration of PRA Using Alon & Martin's Model

Baser Foods is a Turkish subsidiary of Baser Holdings, a family-owned company established in 1973, which also has operations in textiles, plastics, chemicals, and finance. Baser Foods aims to produce the highest quality olive oil and establish a global presence in the branded olive oil industry. In 2001, countries with per capita incomes greater than $2000 per annum and some larger poorer countries with an upper class (who are more likely to change eating habits and be able to afford olive oil) were targets for some planned market expansion.

China was one potential market for expansion but was viewed to be an expensive prospect, as at least a one million Euro marketing campaign would need to be launched to educate consumers on the benefits of olive oil and attempt to change their eating habits. On the other hand, the benefits of the first mover strategy were obvious in a market where the quality of life was improving, GDP was growing, and the population was becoming more educated. Some other markets Baser was considering were Canada and Australia. Although these markets were known to be more stable, the margins that could be earned in them were relatively low, and competition was fierce.

Baser's executives believed that PRA was necessary to see if the potential benefits of expanding into China outweighed the risks. The company commissioned consultants to study the benefits side of the equation while a veteran internal analyst was given the task and budget to perform the PRA. He applied the method described in this chapter to generate the following information.

1. **Symptoms (Perceptions) of Risk Factors that Occur in China:**

   - Internal governmental. Corrupt officials, government regulation, national reforms, inter-regional pushes and pulls

   - **Internal societal.** Demonstrations, strikes, localized regional unrest

   - **Internal economic.** Pockets of poverty, uneven economic development

   - **External governmental.** diplomatic problems, border conflicts

   - **External societal.** Threats of terrorism

   - **External economic.** Change in terms of trade

2. Assign Each Variable a Score:

	Internal		External	
Governmental	Degree of elite repression	-2	Likelihood of political violence	-1
	Degree of elite legitimacy	-2	Involvement in international organizations	2
	Likelihood of regime change	-2	Regulatory restrictions	-2
Societal	Degree of fragmentation	1	World public opinion	1
	Degree of congruent cleavages	1	Disinvestment pressures	2
	Sense of alienation	2	Regional diversity and incongruent interests	0
Economic	Per capita GDP growth	2	Policies on foreign investment	0
	Income distribution	1	Likelihood of debt problems	1
	Likelihood of economic goals being met	-2	Likelihood of currency problems	2

3. Assign a Weight to Each Variable:

Factor importance weights: Olive oil industry		Score
Internal governmental	0.2	-1.2
Internal societal	0.2	0.8
Internal economic	0.15	0.15
External governmental	0.15	-0.15
External societal	0.2	0.6
External economic	0.1	0.3
Total		**0.5**

The analyst calculated the aggregate macropolitical score for China was 0.5 on a scale of -2 to 2. This was viewed to be a moderate but not substantial level of risk. In doing the PRA, the analyst noted that the country had a number of lingering uncertainties that the company would need to consider as it moved ahead with its decisions and plans. Among the issues that were of most concern that the analyst raised for further assessment were the following:

- Will economic growth continue at a healthy rate under the present government?

- Will the current political process be reformed, and will that help or hinder stability?

- What would be the likelihood that indigenous competitors, possibly even state-sponsored ones, would enter the olive oil marketplace?

- Which parts of the company's value chain would be most affected by political risks, for instance, in the hiring of Chinese employees, the use of Chinese distributors, access to appropriate advertising media, and so on?

The executives felt that they were better informed about the option to expand into China and, with some additional recommendations still coming in from other sources, were more confident that they could make the right decision.

Case study adapted from the following sources: Alon & Martin (1998)[3], CIA World Factbook (2005) https://www.cia.gov/library/publications/the-world-factbook/, Leiberthal & Leiberthal (2003)[4], Bremmer (2005)[5], *EIU Country Profile—China* (2005).

Endnotes

[1] CIA World Factbook, 2007.

[2] CIA World Factbook, 2007.

[3] Alon, I. and M.A. Martin, "A Normative Model of Political Risk Assessment," *Multinational Business Review* 6 (1998): 10–20.

[4] Leiberthal, K. and G. Leiberthal (2003). "The Great Transition." *Harvard Business Review* 81: 70-81.

[5] Bremmer, I. (2005). "Managing Risk in an Unstable World." *Harvard Business Review* 83: 51-60.

9

Scenario Analysis

Description and Purpose

A *scenario* is a detailed description of what the future may look like. It is based on a set of assumptions that are critical to an economy's, industry's, or technology's evolution. Scenario analysis is a structured way of developing multiple scenarios that address two common decision-making errors—underprediction and overprediction of change. The objective of scenario analysis is to build a shared baseline for strategic thinking and provide strategic early warning.

Companies facing challenges will especially benefit from scenario planning and analysis when the following conditions are present:

- Uncertainty is high relative to managers' ability to predict or adjust to the future.
- Many costly surprises have occurred in the past.
- The company does not perceive or generate new opportunities.
- The quality of strategic thinking is relatively low.
- The industry has experienced significant change or is about to.
- The company wants a common language and framework without stifling diversity.
- There are strong differences of opinion with multiple opinions having merit.
- The company's competitors are using the technique.

Scenario analysis combines quantitative and qualitative analysis that imagines many possible future scenarios of environmental change; it then reduces these scenarios to a manageable number of possibilities; incorporates sensitivity analysis to determine dependent variable relationships; isolates trends and patterns to counteract blindspots in strategic decision making; and provides a framework for future decisions.

An industry's level of attractiveness (see Chapter 6, "Five Forces Industry Analysis," for additional information) can change as it evolves over time. Predicting how this evolution will unfold is an uncertain task at best. When uncertainty levels are high, scenario analysis can be a helpful way for decision makers and managers to prepare for the future.

A scenario is a story about possible futures built on carefully constructed plots. Industry scenarios develop detailed, internally consistent descriptions of what the industry could look like in the future. The output of a single scenario is one possible configuration for the industry, while a set of scenarios can be used to encompass a wider range of possible futures. The set can then be used to develop and assess potential competitive actions or movements.

There are four general types of approaches to developing scenarios.

Quantitative Method

Computer-Generated Econometric Model

This model attempts to integrate a large number of identified interrelationships between trends. By changing one variable, the downstream effects can be analyzed along with effects on the initial variable.

Qualitative Methods

Intuitive Method

This method rejects the quantitative approach; instead, it stresses the qualitative variables that are thought to disproportionately affect the future. Fundamental trends are identified and projected into the future to try and construct a surprise-free future. This is done by changing some of the trends to explore other possible future outcomes. While this intuitive approach is appealingly simple, the high level of abstraction and lack of systematic application make it less practical and therefore difficult to implement.

Delphi Method

In this method, a panel of both internal and external experts is separately questioned (to reduce peer bias) on current and possible future trends in their particular domain of expertise and/or practice. After several iterations, the results are statistically collated to yield a description of a majority consensus and different opinions. The Delphi approach attempts to determine the sequential causal paths of events and issues that will play out in the future.

Cross-Impact Analysis

This approach also seeks expert opinion but adds the experts' estimation of the probability and time of occurrence of future trends or events. The result is a probability distribution of the likelihood and timeframe of future events that can be leveraged to determine the impact of the removal of one trend or event on the remaining trends or events. Cross-impact analysis focuses on the interrelated dependencies among the various identified events/factors/issues that will impinge on the future.

A mixed scenario analysis is biased toward the qualitative approaches and is a relatively common method employed today. The approach focuses on a qualitative narrative that challenges key assumptions about the future. Initially, a large number of scenarios are developed that are subsequently reduced through either deductive or inductive processes (see Figure 9.1). Through the *deductive reduction* of the number of factors, the general narrative themes of each scenario are considered, followed by the factors that will be dominant influences in each scenario. Alternately, *inductive reduction* involves reducing the factors to a manageable number and then projecting potential future values to multiple combinations of these factors to derive plausible scenarios.

Both deductive and inductive methods offer benefits, but also carry risks. The deductive reduction process allows the analyst to combine many factors into several narratives that describe the future, but it may omit important combinations of factors; hence, a critical scenario may be missed. Inductive reduction, by first reducing the number of factors, may omit an important variable.

To protect against both of these blind spots, both approaches should generally be pursued. Once a manageable number of inputs have been determined, the scenarios can be subjected to more rigorous analysis.

Regardless of which method of scenario analysis is used, five specific scenario types are usually developed:

- **STEEP scenario.** This focuses on events external to the company. Less controllable factors are *social, technological, economic, environmental,* and *political.* The important distinction between a STEEP *scenario* and a traditional STEEP *analysis* is that the STEEP scenario incorporates factor dependencies to yield new competitive conditions that would not be readily identified by the STEEP analysis.
- **Sensitivity scenario.** This has the opposite focal scope of a STEEP scenario in that internal factors controllable by the

company are the subject of analysis. A common example is the spreadsheet approach used by the finance department.

- **Industry scenario.** This focuses on industry-specific issues and trends, which are relevant to the company's business model. It is distinguished from traditional industry analysis in that it analyzes interrelated sequences of trends, events, and issues over time.

- **Diversification scenario.** This focuses on industry-specific issues and trends relevant to potential business models the company may pursue in the future, including those associated with merger and acquisition (M&A) prospects. It is essentially exploratory in nature and seeks to identify current and future trends in the company's industry. This type of scenario analysis also envisions the prospects for industry migration.

- **Public issue scenario.** Often companies that are disproportionately exposed to specific public issues or stakeholder-related events will conduct a public issue scenario. For example, an oil company may choose to center its scenario analysis on energy economics by developing conceivable scenarios of the impact of cartel strength, discovery, conflicts, taxes, and so on of their current and future business models.

The most important factor in the success of any scenario-building program is the active involvement of top management. This will help to make the seemingly abstract intangibles of scenario analysis more tangible to various members of the management team charged with the responsibility of preparing the company for and making decisions about future competition. Another important success factor is the involvement of analysts from diverse backgrounds. In this regard, analysts with strong backgrounds in the liberal arts, humanities, and social sciences can add rich contextual value to the scenario-building process. All else being equal, they will be more attuned to the intangible qualitative factors that often have more bearing on future environments than their more technical or quantitatively oriented colleagues. They are also more likely to act as strategic challengers within the scenario development or analysis process by holding contrarian viewpoints.

Strengths

Scenarios can be used to help determine the sources of competitive advantage or critical success factors as industries evolve. The consequences of each scenario can be used to predict competitors' offensive and defensive moves.

The need for internal consistency in scenario analysis forces the analyst to explicitly address the many interrelated sequences and causal paths that may result in conceivable future scenarios. The test of a good scenario is not whether it portrays the future accurately, but whether it enables a company's decision makers to learn, adapt, and enrich the ongoing "strategic conversation." Through this process of understanding, the company's managers are much better able to grasp the importance of investing in strategic options as a risk contingency strategy. Scenario analysis is one of the best tools to lessen corporate blind spots about the external environment.

It is also extremely flexible in that the relative degree of quantification/qualification or formal/informal characteristics of the scenario approaches taken can be tailored to the individual company's culture and capabilities.

Although scenario analysis often incorporates forecasting techniques from raw analytical inputs, it goes one step further. Through narrative stories, scenario analysis starts where traditional forecasting ends. By including informal assessments of possible future environments, scenario analysis is able to embrace relevant variables that are beyond the quantitative purview of established forecasting techniques.

Scenario analysis is a useful technique because of its ability to reduce an overwhelming amount of data and information. It is structured to help management understand future competitive environments—this is liberating from a procedural point of view because it is not necessary to capture all of the details. It also improves a company's ability to respond nimbly in rapidly changing environments because it

- Ensures that a company is not focusing on catastrophe to the exclusion of opportunity
- Helps a company allocate resources more prudently
- Preserves a company's options
- Ensures that companies look forward, not backward
- Provides companies with the opportunity to rehearse the future

Weaknesses

A potential shortcoming of scenario analysis occurs when companies use it to replace strategy formulation and planning. Scenario analysis allows a company to see the possible consequences of a predetermined strategy, whether it is the company's current or possible future strategy. As such, this is an analytical technique. While it may support, decompose, and formalize a particular strategy, it does not create new strategies.

The tendency to select the scenario that best fits the company's current strengths must be avoided. You need to divorce yourself from this natural tendency and remain objective to the very real possibility of each scenario materializing independent of the company's current competitive position.

The need to get management to agree on scenarios is critical but not always a task that is easy to manage. As scenarios often include both "soft" and "fuzzy" as well as quantitative and analytical information, getting people to agree on their labels can require much effort and time. There are always trade-offs to be made in developing simple versus complex scenarios.

Scenarios are also often appealing due to their conceptual simplicity. A difficult trade-off to make in scenario development is that between "accuracy" and "direction." However, getting managers and decision makers to drill down from base scenarios to the level of competitive and financial implications can be difficult, given that most scenarios are constructed at a broad, macro level.

How to Do It

Despite its story-like qualities, scenario analysis follows systematic and recognizable phases. The process is highly interactive, intense, and imaginative. It begins by isolating the decision to be made, rigorously challenging the mental maps that shape one's perceptions, and hunting and gathering information, often from unorthodox sources.

These phases are summarized in Figure 9.1.

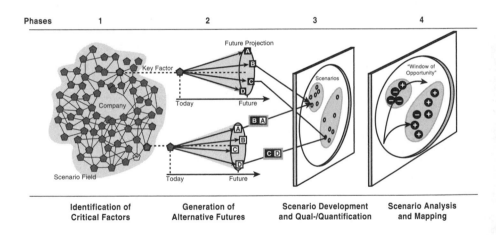

Figure 9.1 Four phases of scenario development

Adapted from A. Fink, A. Siebe, and J. Kuhle, "How Scenarios Support Strategic Early Warning Processes," *Foresight* 6(3), 2004: 173–185.

Although there is no single correct way to conduct scenario analysis, several practical guidelines have been developed from collective experience with this approach. The process we describe next for developing scenarios is the one promoted most notably by Schoemaker.[1]

1. *Define the scope of the analysis.* Set the timeframe and the scope of the analysis in terms of products, markets, customer groups, technologies, or geographic areas. The timeframe is dependent on several factors, including industry or product life cycles, political elections, competitors' planning horizons, rate of technological change, economic cycles, and so on. Once the appropriate timeframe has been determined, ask what knowledge would be of the highest value to your company at that point in time.

2. *Identify the major stakeholders.* What parties will have an interest in the development of issues of importance in the future? Who will be affected by these parties, and who will affect them? Identify the stakeholders' current roles, interests, and power positions and then assess how they have changed over time.

3. *Identify basic trends.* What industry and STEEP trends are likely to affect the issues you identified in the first step? Briefly explain each trend, including how (positively, negatively, or neutrally) and why it influences your company. Those trends in which there is disagreement over their likely continuation are dealt with in the following step.

4. *Identify uncertainties.* What outcomes and events are uncertain or will significantly affect the issues you are concerned about? For each uncertainty, determine possible outcomes (that is, legislation passed or defeated or technology developed or not developed). Also attempt to determine whether relationships exist among these uncertainties and rule out those combinations that are implausible (for example, steadily increasing government and private debt and deficits with steadily declining interest rates).

5. ***Construct initial scenario themes.*** Several approaches can be utilized, including (a) selecting the top two uncertainties and evaluating them; (b) clustering various strings of possible outcomes around high versus low continuity, degree of preparedness, turmoil and so on; or (c) identifying extreme worlds by putting all positive elements in one scenario and all negative elements in another.

6. ***Check for consistency and plausibility.*** Assess the following: Are the trends compatible within the chosen timeframe? If not, remove those trends that do not fit. Next, do the scenarios combine outcomes of uncertainties that indeed fit together? If not, eliminate that scenario. Lastly, are the major stakeholders placed in positions they do not like and can change? If so, your scenario will evolve into another one.

7. ***Develop learning scenarios.*** Some general themes should have emerged from performing the previous steps. Your goal is to identify themes that are strategically relevant and then organize the possible trends and outcomes around these themes. Although the trends appear in each scenario, they should be given more or less weight or attention in different scenarios as appropriate.

8. ***Identify research needs.*** You might need to delve more deeply into your blind spots and improve your understanding of uncertainties and trends; for example, consider if you really understand how stakeholders are likely to behave in a particular scenario.

9. ***Develop quantitative models.*** Re-examine the internal consistencies of the scenarios and assess whether certain interactions need to be formalized via a quantitative model. The models can help to quantify the consequences of various scenarios and keep managers from straying toward implausible scenarios.

10. ***Evolve toward decision scenarios.*** Iteratively converge toward scenarios that you will eventually use to test your strategies and generate innovative ideas. Ask yourself whether the scenarios address the real issues facing your company and

whether they will spur the creativity and appreciation of your company's decision makers.

These steps should ideally culminate in three or four carefully constructed scenario plots. If the scenarios are to function as learning tools, the lessons they teach must be based on issues that are critical to the success of the decision. Only a few scenarios can be fully developed and remembered, and each should represent a plausible alternative future, not a best case, worst case and most likely continuum. Once the scenarios have been fleshed out and made into a narrative, the team identifies their implications and the leading indicators to be monitored on an ongoing basis.

This can also be represented in a scenario matrix as follows:

Environmental Uncertainty					
Development of External Scenarios					
		External Scenario A	External Scenario B	External Scenario C	External Scenario D	External Scenario F
	Strategy Scenario 1	+	+ +	●	+ +	— —
	Strategy Scenario 2	+ +	+	+	+ +	+ +
Internal Uncertainty / Development of Strategy Scenarios	Strategy Scenario 3	— —	+ +	+	●	+
	Strategy Scenario 4	+ +	●	— —	●	+ +
	Strategy Scenario 5	—	—	+ +	+	—

Is the strategic scenario robust against alternative conditions?

Which is the best strategy (scenario) within a specific external development?

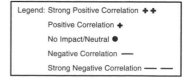

Legend: Strong Positive Correlation + +
Positive Correlation +
No Impact/Neutral ●
Negative Correlation —
Strong Negative Correlation — —

Figure 9.2 Scenario matrix

Adapted from A. Fink, A. Siebe, and J. Kuhle, "How Scenarios Support Strategic Early Warning Processes," *Foresight* 6(3), 2004: 173–185.

Once the number of scenario "plots" has been decided upon, the strategic intent of the company must be determined. It is here that scenario analysis ends and strategic decision making begins. Essentially, three options are open to the company when dealing with future uncertainty.

- **Shape the future.** The most intense stance is for the company to plan to be a shape-shifter by defining the competitive parameters of future scenario(s) by betting on future trends (such as technological discontinuities or the erosion of mobility barriers).

- **Adapt to the future.** This is a benchmarking approach that puts the company in a position of operational excellence to capitalize on trends as soon as they develop.

- **Strategic options.** This is a more conservative, proactive strategy that invests the minimal amount necessary to acquire or otherwise purchase strategic options, while avoiding overt vulnerability.

These three strategic opportunities offer different levels of risk and hence different levels of potential reward.

Unlike traditional forecasting or market research, scenarios present alternative images instead of extrapolating current trends from the present. Scenarios also embrace qualitative perspectives and the potential for sharp discontinuities that econometric and other stable-state quantitative models exclude. Consequently, creating scenarios requires managers to question their broadest assumptions about the way the world works so that they can anticipate decisions that might otherwise be missed or denied. Within the company, scenarios provide a common vocabulary and an effective basis for communicating complicated conditions and options.

Good scenarios are plausible and can be surprising, and they should have the power to break old stereotypes. By using scenarios you and your participating colleagues are rehearsing the future; and by recognizing the warning signs and the drama that is unfolding, you can avoid surprises, adapt, and act effectively. Decisions that have been pretested against a range of possible futures are more likely to stand the test of time and produce robust and resilient plans of action. Ultimately, the end result of scenario analysis is not a more accurate picture of tomorrow, but better decisions today.

Case Study

Clinical Trial Disclosure and the Impact/Probability Matrix

An impact/probability matrix was put to use for a group of pharmaceutical industry decision makers who were concerned about clinical trials and their disclosure to the public. In the past, drug companies have been able to conduct clinical trials to learn about the drugs they are developing or marketing, but have been under no obligation to publish their findings.

Over the past couple of years, several events have led government agencies to call for mandatory disclosure of trial data. Pharmaceutical maker GlaxoSmithKline (GSK) was sued by New York Attorney General Eliot Spitzer in 2004 for fraudulently withholding information on trials on the use of the antidepressant Paxil in children. As part of its settlement, the company is disclosing all trials, regardless of outcome, on a public database. This has spurred many stakeholders, from medical journal editors to the U.S. Congress, to consider permanent, industry-wide, mandatory databases for all trials so that companies can no longer hide unflattering data. Proponents argue that this would improve the access that doctors and patients have to information about drugs.

For the industry decision makers, we used an impact/probability matrix to explore how much disclosure might be mandated and how such mandates would change strategies at pharmaceutical companies. The impact/probability matrix in Figure 9.3 shows how the scenarios played out.

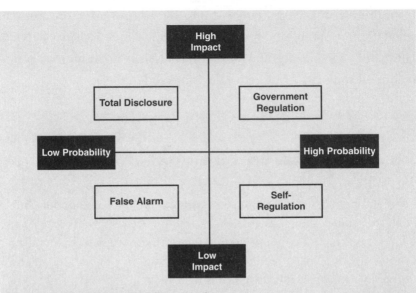

Figure 9.3 Impact/probability matrix

Scenario 1: False Alarm—Low Probability, Low Impact (Flash in the Pan)

American business has a short attention span, and there are sometimes fads and short-lived obsessions that quickly disappear. In the *false alarm* scenario, the news cycle churns on, and the media gets tired of discussing something as arcane as clinical trial design and disclosure. Political interest, too, moves on when the election year is over.

In this scenario, the politicians have scored their victories and have moved on to reform industries other than pharmaceuticals. The election year passes, and no political points are left to win. The news media finds that the only details of the story left to debate are so specialized and complicated that only pharmaceutical company executives, physicians, and FDA regulators are willing to tune in.

This scenario is unlikely, as aging Americans, Medicare budget battles, and rising drug costs keep pressure on all aspects of the pharmaceutical business. The public probably will not turn away at this point.

Scenario 2: Self-Regulation—High Probability, Low Impact (Business as Usual)

If no additional major events occur, and pharmaceutical companies decide to increase their own disclosure, the government may allow the industry to police itself regarding disclosure of information to the public. This is the low-government-intervention scenario—*self-regulation*.

In this scenario, pharmaceutical companies all agree to post the results of completed Phase III clinical trials, which are material to understanding marketed drugs. Phase II and III clinical trials of compounds not yet on the market will be conducted without any requirement for disclosure, though often the investment community will learn of these so as to understand the impacts of product R&D on a company's future.

Scenario 3: Government Regulation—High Probability, High Impact (Brewing Storm)

The scenario with the greatest likelihood and impact for the industry is where *government regulations* mandate the disclosure of clinical trials.

In this scenario, legal actions continue to pile up, along with continued pressure on the healthcare industry in general.

The voluntary database PhRMA (Pharmaceutical Research and Manufacturers of America) fails to become a useful tool because of a lack of voluntary participation. Public and government discontent continues to grow.

To avoid further legal action, drug companies agree to a government-run database that discloses data on all Phase III clinical trials, regardless of their results. There would be penalties for lack of disclosure.

Scenario 4: Total Disclosure—Low Probability, High Impact (Wild Card)

If there are more scandals involving drug safety or obfuscation of trial data, the public could become so distrustful of the pharmaceutical industry that government agencies might move to demand full registration of all research activities—from preclinical to Phase III trials and through to a new drug application, irrespective of the market potential of the drugs—*total disclosure*.

All participation would be mandatory. Other drug company activities would likely be monitored as well, including what the sales representatives tell prospective customers and how much doctors are paid to provide clinical information.

Business Implications of These Scenarios

The impact/probability matrix has delineated a range of scenarios, all with varying degrees of disclosure imposed on the pharmaceutical industry.

The next step is to look at the potential impact of these scenarios. Here are a few:

- **Silence might win.** If the movement toward more public disclosure of drug-trial results is only a flash in the pan, then smart companies will be followers, not leaders. If GSK and Eli Lilly provide a clinical trial database with full disclosure, they will have to live with the potentially negative competitive consequences, while other companies will still have options.

- **Disclosure becomes a way of life.** We could see a new era of government oversight in pharmaceutical industry regulation. There may be new regulatory boards added to government agencies, and companies might need to augment their government relations departments because the regulations are now mandatory.

- **First to market is not always preferable; fast followers gain new advantage.** The new era of disclosure will change how companies come first to market. It is conventional wisdom that the first to market gets increased brand recognition. Now there is a trade-off. Later entries into markets may be able to structure Phase III trial programs more cheaply because companies will learn from their competitors about blind alleys to avoid.

- **Learn from every lab in the world.** There will be a loss of secrecy, as competitors can observe trial design, patient populations, endpoints, and eventually results. Drug companies will be able to reap greater efficiencies as they learn from others. The total cost of drug development could be reduced as competing laboratories avoid duplicating each other's mistakes and improve the design of their clinical trials.

- **Fewer studies.** Companies may potentially limit studies if all trials must be registered and all results disclosed. A faulty or even exploratory trial design could result in immediate criticism by one's competitors. Post-marketing studies would typically be more open, but head-to-head trials will instantly signal to a competitor an attack on its market share. Head-to-head studies may become riskier, as it would be less possible to conduct trails such as the PROVE IT statin study by Bristol-Myers Squibb, which inadvertently showed the superiority of Pfizer's Lipitor. Pharmaceutical companies may adopt a more targeted approach.

- **More successful studies.** Even well-designed trials may result in unfavorable results due to poor enrollment, uncertain methodology, or endpoints of disease that are not universally accepted. Learning from the experiences of other laboratories could help companies avoid the pitfalls.

Case study summarized from Eric Garland, "Scenarios in Practice: Futuring in the Pharmaceutical Industry," *The Futurist*, January–February 2006: 30–34.

Endnote

[1]Schoemaker, P. J. H., "How to Link Strategic Vision to Core Capabilities," *Sloan Management Review* 34(1), 1992a: 67–81; "Multiple Scenario Development: Its Conceptual and Behavioral Foundation," *Strategic Management Journal* 14, 1992b: 193–213; and "Scenario Planning: A Tool for Strategic Thinking," *Sloan Management Review* 36(2), 1995: 25–39.

10

Macroenvironmental (STEEP/PEST) Analysis

Description and Purpose

This chapter focuses on the social, technological, economic, ecological, and political/legal (STEEP) aspects of the environment that can affect the competitiveness of industries and companies (also sometimes referred to as political, economic, social, technological (PEST) analysis). These factors are generally considered to be beyond the direct influence of an individual company.

For the purposes of this chapter and for ease of understanding, we will refer to this technique as STEEP, although you can simplify the technique to PEST factors.

Although many organizations recognize the importance of the environment, all too often this analysis ends up making a small or minimal contribution to strategy analysis and formulation. This can be because the organization views the environment as being too uncertain to do anything about or because many environmental factors have delayed or indirect effects on the organization and often escape the notice of managers who are more concerned with day-to-day operations.

Analysts commonly segment the environment into three distinct levels: the general environment, the operating environment, and the internal environment.

Figure 10.1 illustrates the relationship of each of these levels with each other and the organization. This book as a whole provides techniques that allow you to understand things happening at all three levels.

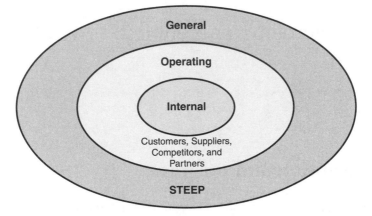

Figure 10.1 The three levels of the environment

Managers must be aware of these environmental levels, know what factors they include, and try to understand how each factor and the relationships among the factors affect organizational performance. The STEEP technique described in this chapter will especially help you to understand the general environmental level.

The general environment is broad in scope and has long-term implications for the organization and its strategies. These implications are usually understood to be beyond the direct influence of an organization—for example the role of government and government legislation on an industry.

The general environment is broken down into sub-categories or segments. One effective segmentation is known as the STEEP categorization scheme. As described earlier, it also comes under different names, including things like PEST, PESTLE, SEPTember, STEEPLES, and so on. More important than which of these schemes is chosen, is to recognize that the primary purpose of these segments or subcategories is to avoid overlooking major aspects of the general environment in your overall analysis.

Table 10.1 shows several key variables that would be present under each individual STEEP factor as identified in Figure 10.2. The STEEP sectors are not mutually exclusive—the lines between the categories remain fluid. Issues, events, or stakeholders can actually traverse several sectors at once.

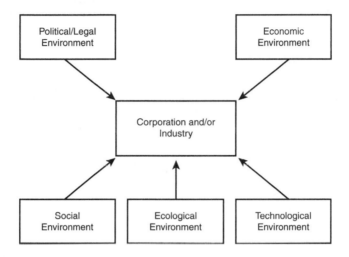

Figure 10.2 The elements of STEEP analysis

Environmental conditions affect the entire strategic management process. Organizations do not operate in a vacuum, and a key to effective strategic management is to make decisions that will enable actions to correspond positively with the context in which those actions will ultimately take place. To some degree, an organization's internal conditions, in particular its strengths, weaknesses, resources, or capabilities, will determine the action. On the other hand, the action is often largely dictated by external factors. To some extent, the company can shape the environment to its advantage or react in ways that disadvantage it less than its competitors.

TABLE 10.1 Key STEEP Variables

Social	Technological	Ecological	Economic	Political/ Legal
Ideological characteristics	Patents held	Air and water quality	GDP growth rates	Policies of political parties
Types of union organizations	R&D budgets	Recycling capacity	Exchange reserves	Activism of regulatory agencies
Income gaps among social segments	Number of colleges and universities in a region	Sources of power	Rate of inflation	Presence of property protection laws
Percentage of population in economic and social segments	Pace of technological change	Stage of evolution in the product life cycle	Income distribution levels and bands	Ability to influence political decision making
Value systems for social classes	Presence of technology clusters	Pollution levels	Interest rates	Voting rates and trends
Cultural background of citizens	Pace of process or product improvements	Substitutability of raw materials	Small business lending levels	Nature of power and decision-making structures
Birth and death rates	Bandwidth capacity	Level of environmental regulation	Balance of payments	Public opinion

Strengths

The key strength of environmental analysis is that it has the explicit task of leading executive thinking beyond current activities and short-term horizons, while still making frequent and sensible links to current and shorter term activities to retain credibility. To be successful, environmental analysis needs to be linked conceptually and practically to current planning operations—thus it is important to involve key organizational planners in the environmental analysis.

The organization's process of strategy formulation is considerably weakened unless it has a filtering process that allows it to establish the importance and relevance of external developments. The STEEP technique allows this to happen.

The organization's decision makers must also develop a structured way of identifying and analyzing relevant trends, events, and stakeholder expectations in the STEEP environment, including the systematic assessment of environmental change on the company's businesses and action plans. This can be accomplished at an organization-wide policy level or in a functionally focused way (for example, new products for marketing managers or lobbying strategies for government affairs managers).

An organization's success or failure can substantially depend on how accurately its decision makers read the environment and respond to it. Therefore, managers must think carefully about who should gather the information and how to structure its flow and use—cross-functional teams of internal specialists can often perform environmental analysis effectively. Having the support and encouragement of top management is an important success factor, as is having appropriate systems established to support the effort.

For environmental analysis to fulfill its purpose, it must "fit" the organization's strategy, culture, planning processes, and the unique styles of its decision makers.

Successful environmental analysis also needs to be responsive to the information needs of decision makers. As such, these information needs may change over time, and you will need to adjust the environmental analysis in accordance with such changes.

Effective environmental analysis will have a positive effect on competitive performance if proper actions are taken and proper evaluations are made. Timely actions will yield good results over an extended period of time.

Weaknesses

Several empirical studies have shown that the STEEP method of environmental analysis is difficult to do effectively over time. Different types of environmental contexts (for example, dynamic or placid, simple or complex, and continuous or discontinuous) also impact its effectiveness.

Problems in environmental analysis tend to fall within several categories:

- **Interpretation.** Organizational decision makers often have difficulties in conceptualizing or defining what their environment is, making it difficult to interpret the specific kinds of impact the environmental variables will have and the nature of effective responses that the organization may choose to pursue. Weaknesses in interpreting environmental factors include being able to structure meaningful studies, showing financial impact, synthesizing short and long-term implications, a lack of senior management involvement in the analysis, difficulties in translating potential opportunities into action plans, and appropriating the time and resources required to do accurate analysis.

- **Inaccuracy and uncertainty.** Problems experienced here include inaccuracies in analytical output and lack of faith in the results due to the presence of too many ambiguities and uncertainties or a combination of both. This can be a result of difficulties in depicting environmental events and trends and properly characterizing uncertainties in meaningful terms as well as difficulties in accurately forecasting the effects of STEEP forces and the social and technological evolution and trends.

- **Short-term orientation.** Many decision makers dislike spending "real" money today for speculative results tomorrow and are primarily concerned with short-term matters. Many of the variables in the STEEP segments take numerous years to evolve, frequently far outlasting the analysts and decision makers in the organizations who need to understand them.

- **Lack of acceptance.** Not accepting the value of environmental analysis can be due to management's lack of understanding of its value, difficulties in encouraging line managers to utilize its outputs, resistance to changing forecasting methods, and presumptions among managers that they are already experts in the implementation and management of this process. Another related issue is the failure to link the STEEP analysis to competitive implications. A key goal of using this technique should always be the identification of competitive implications for the organization based on the environment analysis.

- **Misperceptions.** Management's limited scope or invalid perceptions about the environment; for example, thinking in country terms as opposed to global terms.

- **Diversified businesses.** Human limitations, prior experience, and bias affect environmental analysis. This is especially true in multinational environments where home-country biases and attitudes often lead organizations to superimpose their own experiences, views, and understanding on variables that do not act in ways suggested or supported by the STEEP factors.

How to Do It

The environmental boundaries you define will bind the breadth, depth, and forecasting horizon of the analysis. Breadth refers to the topical coverage of the environmental data collected; depth determines the level of detail in the STEEP data being sought and analyzed; and forecasting horizons will usually span the short, medium, and longer terms of time, as dictated by the relevant organization's specific environment.

To establish environmental boundaries, examine the organization's strategic plans with respect to its geographic reach (where it does and does not compete), its product or service scope (segments, categories), its time horizon for returns on fixed resource commitments, technology and innovation, sources of its resources (human, capital, other financial and raw materials), regulatory issues, and flexibility. Note that the process will be constrained by the resources available and dedicated to performing the task.

Once the environmental boundaries have been defined, the five STEEP segments can be analyzed by addressing the following five-step process:

1. Understand the segment of the environment being analyzed.
2. Understand interrelationships between trends.
3. Relate trends to issues.
4. Forecast the future direction of issues.
5. Derive implications.

Step 1: Understand the Segment of the Environment Being Analyzed

What are the current key events and trends within the segment? Events are important occurrences in the different STEEP domains. Trends are the general tendency for events to occur and the course of those events. For example, within the social segment, you would look to capture trends surrounding work and leisure, consumption and savings, education, travel, religious activities, and household work.

What is the evidence supporting the existence of these trends? It is important that data or evidence underlying the existence of trends is captured so as to facilitate continued monitoring and forecasting of the trend's direction and evolution.

How have the trends evolved historically? Like industries, products, and organizations, trends have life cycles with identifiable stages—they emerge, develop, peak, and decline. You need to identify where a trend is in its life cycle. An understanding of the cycle of trends is critical in identifying their subsequent evolution.

What is the nature and degree of change or turbulence within trends? Trends fluctuate according to their rate of evolution, magnitude, and fractionation. Rate of change in a trend requires you to focus on whether the trend is accelerating, decelerating, or remaining static in its life cycle. Magnitude looks at the degree of spread associated with a trend and whether it is affecting larger or smaller groups to greater or lesser degrees. Fractionation looks at the relationship of the trend with other trends to see whether the focal trend is impacting or being impacted by other trends.

What kind of impacts do the trends have for the organization? Conceptually, there are three different kinds of impact that trends may have for the organization:

- **Negative impacts.** These are associated with threats to the organization's ability to achieve its goals. They may also prevent the organization from acting upon its current strategy, increase its risks associated with moving forward with the existing strategy, increase the level of resources required to implement the strategy, or suggest that a strategy is no longer appropriate.

- **Positive impacts.** These are associated with opportunities for the organization to achieve its goals. The trends may support or strengthen existing strategies, may increase the likelihood of the organization being able to implement its planned strategy, or suggest a new opportunity that can be exploited if one or more strategies were changed within the framework of the organization's existing mission.

- **Neutral or zero impacts.** These may be stabilizing or irrelevant forces and may also increase the confidence decision makers have in their strategies.

Step 2: Understand Interrelationships Between Trends

What are the interrelationships between trends? An understanding of the interrelationships requires you to identify the impact between the different STEEP segments and subsegments. Look for areas where trends are suggesting redefinitions or changes from the expected evolutionary path or where they are reinforcing one another.

What are the conflicts between trends? Trends often push in opposite directions and counteract one another. For example, people are becoming more committed to their work at the same time that they are seeking more family time outside of the workplace.

Step 3: Relate Trends to Issues

Not all trends are of equal importance to an organization or an industry. Some trends will affect an organization directly, while others might only have a tangential effect, depending on how they interact with the organization's strategy and its execution. The astute analyst will identify those trends and combinations of trends that are likely to have the highest impact on the organization's goals. The most critical ones are defined as "issues" for the organization. This is where STEEP and issue analysis (see Chapter 7) find complementarities.

Step 4: Forecast the Future Direction of Issues

Assess the underlying forces. Forecasting the future evolution of a trend or set of trends within an "issue" requires analyzing the driving forces behind the issue. You must be able to distinguish between symptoms and causes—a difficult task, as often the driving forces work against one another and push simultaneously in multiple directions. Once the causes are accurately identified, alternative projections of the issue's evolution can be developed.

Make alternative projections of the issues. To avoid the limitations created by single forecasts, it is useful to develop multiple projections or scenarios. Each of these scenarios will represent a differing view of the future that is developed around clearly identified trends. For example, identify a best case, worst case, and neutral case scenario for issue development. Then subject the scenario to a set of questions to test its veracity, such as: What underlying forces are propelling the trends? What is the probability or likelihood that they will continue?

How strong is the evidence that its component trends are accurate? Do the interrelationships among the trends make sense? This is where STEEP and scenario analysis (see Chapter 9) find complementarities.

Step 5: Derive Implications

Macroenvironmental analysis needs to make a contribution to and serve as an input to the organization's strategic planning. Implications should be focused on three levels, the following in particular:

1. The structural forces surrounding your industry and any strategic groups within the industry

2. How they affect your organization's strategy

3. How they are expected to affect competitors' strategies

This assessment should provide the key inputs in determining what future strategies might be.

Case Study

Life and Death of Brands

Some of the major brands that currently adorn our homes and offices will face decline and death in the future. Brands, as with every product and service, are affected and/or influenced by a combination of internal (micro) and external (macro) environmental factors. For example, consider the STEEP elements and their influence on brands and the marketplace:

Societal

Products and the brand names associated with them may become socially unacceptable. People are also generally more observant of newer or more hyped/exciting developments, as opposed to long-standing, comfortable ones. Equally, consumer tastes change and the brand may have lagged behind, thus risking a rapid decline. In other words, the organization has failed to consider the health of the brand.

Technological

Technology can create radical change and create great disruptions or distortions in pre-existing markets. The introduction of the Internet has seen the demise of the fax machine and caused great havoc to traditional recording media like LPs, cassette tapes, or compact discs. What products and/or services will nanotechnology change?

Economic

A recession can have a significant effect on whether current customers can afford to continue purchasing certain types of branded products, particularly luxury or leisure-oriented ones that are generally ascribed to discretionary income categories. Equally, a rise in raw material costs, such as oil, will affect the financial performance of a brand. If there is long-term economic instability, the future of the brand may be in jeopardy. A tip worth keeping in mind is that when looking at economic issues, always look at global economic issues.

Environmental

Global warming will impact brands in the future and may already be doing so at present in ways yet difficult to pinpoint. Automotive manufacturers, no matter where they are in the world, will need to consider replacing the current combustion engine, not to mention more deeply consider the life cycles of their products far beyond their useful functional life (cradle to grave thinking). Companies that have invested in alternative power supplies, such as fuel cells, will most likely increase the longevity of their brands.

Political

If a country is politically unstable, it is likely to be or to become economically unstable. This can have major impact on a brand that is limited to one particular country market. If a brand has regional or international presence, it may be buffered or otherwise protected within those additional markets.

The political segment also includes acts of terrorism. The destruction of a Pam Am flight over Lockerbie in Scotland signaled the end of a once dominant international brand.

Legal

This is often linked to the political situation within a market. Changes in legislation can have serious effects on brand longevity. This can be seen with various tobacco brands that have seen markets reduced due to legislation that restricts/prevents promotion or utilization of the brands. In some cases, companies have diversified into different product ranges, keeping the ability to leverage or trade on their brand name.

By understanding these influencing factors, an organization can review its brand position within the marketplace. Moreover, it can attempt to forecast or scenario-plan possible outcomes for its brands, depending on the implication of the trends of the STEEP factors. For example, as mentioned, a tobacco brand facing increasing global promotion and distribution restrictions might seek to diversify into other business areas. It might be able to leverage and re-energize an existing brand name to develop new market opportunities. Marlboro diversified into a range of clothing distributed through its own stores.

Case study adapted from J. Groucutt, "The Life, Death and Resuscitation of Brands," *Handbook of Business Strategy* 2006: 101–106.

11

SWOT Analysis

Description and Purpose

SWOT (strengths, weaknesses, opportunities, and threats) analysis is used to evaluate the fit between a company's internal resources and capabilities (that is, its strengths and weaknesses) and external possibilities (that is, opportunities and threats).

A company has a greater degree of practical control over its internal environment—which includes resources, culture, operating systems, staffing practices, and the personal values of the company's managers. These areas are generally subject to the discretionary decision making of the organization's executives.

A company has lesser control over its external environment—which includes market demand; the degree of market saturation; government policies; economic conditions; social, cultural, and ethical developments; technological developments; ecological developments (see Chapter 10 for more about STEEP); and factors making up Porter's Five Forces (that is, intensity of rivalry, threat of new entrants, threat of substitute products, bargaining power of buyers, and bargaining power of suppliers). Refer to Chapter 6 for a detailed discussion of the Five Forces model, also known as industry analysis.

Ken Andrews, regarded as the pioneer of SWOT analysis, in 1971 was one of the first strategy theorists to formally describe the concept of strategic fit between a company's internal environment (its resources and capabilities) and its external environment. He claimed a SWOT analysis could identify the best way for a company to use its strengths to exploit opportunities and to defend both its strengths and weaknesses against external threats. Figure 11.1 demonstrates the thinking and strategic questioning behind the SWOT technique. Figure 11.2 identifies the SWOT process. In reality, most managers generally only undertake Part A—and may not even do that facet properly.

SWOT can be applied to many areas of a company, including products, divisions, and services. The simplicity and ease of use of this model has made it a very popular technique, particularly for determining a company's ability to deal with its environment. However, it is also one of the most misused and poorly understood methods of analysis.

SWOT is a common technique for analyzing and exploring a company's situation and is often popularly thought of as "situation analysis." It guides executives in developing an overall marketplace context for the company.

This analysis consists of both an external and internal component and provides management with an overview and understanding of the forces, trends, and characteristics of a particular market. The insights from this analysis are then used to assist managers to make informed choices about what actions to take to maintain a company's comparative advantage (that is, developing its strengths while minimizing its weaknesses) and increase its ability to achieve its goals and objectives.

A company analyzes its external environment to identify both present and future opportunities and threats that could influence its competitive ability.

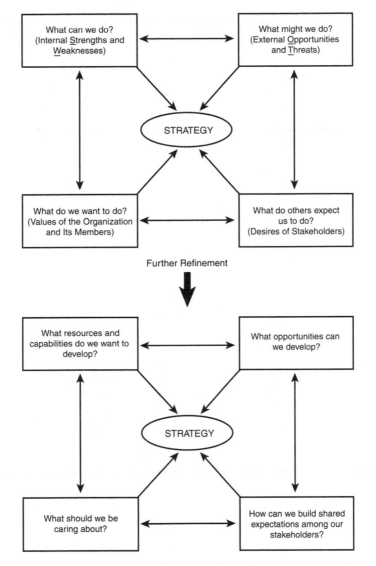

Figure 11.1 The roots of SWOT: key questions that guide strategic choice

Adapted from James G. Clawson, Strategic Thinking (University of Virginia Graduate School of Management, UVA-BP-0391, 1998) p.4-5, Darden Graduate Business School Foundation, Charlottesville: VA.

Figure 11.2—Part A The SWOT technique: identifying, analyzing, and ranking strategic issues

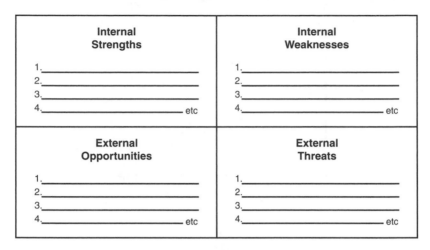

Figure 11.2—Part B Specification of SWOT variables and development of strategy to improve matches

		Internal Factors	
		Strengths	**Weaknesses**
External Factors	**Opportunities**	Internal Strengths Matched with External Opportunities 1. 2. 3. 4.	Internal Weaknesses Matched with External Opportunities 1. 2. 3. 4.
	Threats	Internal Strengths Matched with External Threats 1. 2. 3. 4.	Internal Weaknesses Matched with External Threats 1. 2. 3. 4.

COMPETITIVE ADVANTAGE

A company's external environment consists of two main areas, including its

- **Operating environment that relates to a particular industry.** Suppliers, competitors, customers, labor, and international components.
- **General environment.** The social, technological, economic, environmental, and political/legal (STEEP) components within which the industry and the company are situated.

Environmental analysis can help managers answer the following critical questions:

- What are the competitive forces in our industry, and how strongly will they affect us?
- What factors are affecting competition?
- What are competitors' assumptions about the changing environment?
- What environmental factors are vital to our competitive success?
- Is the industry's environment attractive or unattractive now, and how will it look in the future?

A company's internal operating environment is equally important. To better understand a company's abilities, a manager needs to look at things such as its cost drivers, resources, and capabilities.

Overall, a SWOT analysis enables managers to better understand and respond to the factors that can have the greatest impact on a company's performance. These factors are called the company's *strategic issues*. A strategic issue exists either inside or outside the company and is likely to have a major and long-term impact on the ability of the company to meet its competitive objectives. Strategic issues typically impact across the entire company and require greater resources to effectively address them.

Information derived from a SWOT analysis assists in the identification of strategic issues—such as new technologies, market trends, new competitors, and customer satisfaction trends. These in turn require interpretation and translation, as well as the formulation and execution of strategies to address them.

However, a company's internal and external environment changes over time. Vigilant review of strengths, weaknesses, opportunities, and threats is required to deal with these ever-changing issues.

Strengths

The SWOT technique is easy to use for organizing large amounts of information and for applying a general framework to understand and manage the environment in which a company operates. It can be used to analyze a variety of issues, including individuals, teams, projects, products, services, functional areas (such as accounting, marketing, production, and sales), business units, and corporations. It works equally well for for-profit and not-for-profit companies. It can provide insight into why a particular company has been successful or unsuccessful in carrying out its strategy.

Compared to other techniques, it does not require a great deal of external information, financial resources, or IT capabilities. It provides an effective framework for identifying the critical issues when dealing with complex situations in a short amount of time.

It enables managers to focus on the issues that have the most impact on the company and those which can be effectively dealt with by their capabilities and resources. It also provides a guide for managers to analyze the options available to them in responding to their competitive environments and assists in evaluating their core capabilities, competencies, and resources.

It can be effective for team building when different areas of the business, such as marketing, production, and finance undertake a SWOT together. Managers, for example, can review the strengths, weaknesses, opportunities, and threats closest to their specialties and alert colleagues from other departments and senior executives to the issues they see as critical to the SWOT.

The process of collecting, interpreting, and organizing the many sources of information onto the SWOT grid (see Figure 11.2) also provides an excellent base from which to guide further strategic analysis.

Weaknesses

The SWOT technique masks a great deal of complexity. The primary concern for managers is the collection and interpretation of what can be a large amount of information concerning environmental factors and then deciding what to do in response to it. Interpretation of the information will likely differ between individual managers—for example, one manager may see the loosening of government-imposed trade barriers between nations as a market expansion opportunity, whereas another may see it as a threat due to competition that might ensue. This far too easily confused set of opportunities and threats is a commonly experienced problem.

Only broadly generalized recommendations are typically offered from a SWOT analysis, such as moving the company away from threats; matching the company's strengths with opportunities; or defending against the weaknesses through divestment or investment. It is also limited in its ability to help a company identify specific actions to follow. It provides little guidance relative to strategy execution.

The data used tends to be qualitative rather than quantitative—and focuses on delivering reactive rather than proactive strategies. Weaknesses tend to be more broadly identified, while strengths tend to be more narrowly defined. In fact, managers are frequently too optimistic in their assessment of a company's strengths and opportunities versus their weaknesses and threats. Weaknesses are often ignored entirely, more common in those situations where the SWOT is performed under conditions of political resource scarcity or infighting.

It often fails because of managers' blind spots regarding the company's capabilities (see Chapter 10 in our book *Strategic and Competitive Analysis* for a detailed treatment of blind spot analysis). Due to the subjective nature of this process, it may be appropriate for an outsider to assist managers with the SWOT to ensure biases are kept at a minimum. Otherwise, the results of your SWOT analysis will not be used to inform and drive strategy but will be viewed as a "**S**ubstantial **W**aste **O**f **T**ime," an outcome you should be careful to avoid!

How to Do It

The process for gathering and interpreting information in a SWOT analysis should be an interrelated and reinforcing process of consultation and verification with executives, functional experts, and team members. Additionally, acquiring and utilizing the perceptions of customers can also be highly illuminating in this process.

Step 1: List and Evaluate SWOT Elements

The first step involves listing and evaluating the company's strengths, weaknesses, opportunities, and threats.

- **Strengths** are those factors that make a company more competitive than its rivals. It is where the company has an advantage over or superior assets to the competition. A strength is meaningful only when it is useful to satisfy an existing or prospective customer need. When this is the case, that strength becomes a capability. Strengths are, in effect, capabilities and resources that the company can use effectively to achieve its performance objectives. When addressing strengths, it is important to keep to the facts and not get caught up in cultural biases or blind spots.

- **Weaknesses** are limitations, faults, or defects within the company that can prevent it from achieving its objectives. It is when the company performs poorly or has inferior capabilities or resources to the competition. While some weaknesses may be relatively harmless, those that relate to specific existing or future customer needs should be minimized if possible. Again, you need to be mindful of blind spots.

- **Opportunities** relate to any favorable current or prospective situation in the external environment, such as a trend, change, or overlooked need that supports a product or service and permits the company to enhance its competitive position.

- **Threats** include any unfavorable situation, trend, or impending change in the external environment that currently or potentially damages or threatens the company's ability to compete.

You may want to refer to such techniques as the Value Chain, Porter's Five Forces, or STEEP to ensure that you are identifying a broad range of strengths, weaknesses, opportunities, and threats both for now and in the future.

Although many published SWOT analyses stop at the end of this step, all that you have really done is produce four separate lists of factors. We describe this interim output as "four bunches of bullet points" that have undergone only minimal thought or transformation. This is not analysis in any professional sense and should never be allowed to substitute for constructive analysis. The astute analyst will recognize this step is only a starting point and will proceed with the following steps.

Step 2: Analyze and Rank Strategic Factors

This step of the SWOT analysis will look similar to Figure 11.2 Part A—a ranked list (by aspects such as importance or magnitude) of factors classified as internal strengths and weaknesses and external opportunities and threats. It is important to widely share criteria for the ranking so that the company can better understand the basis upon which they are prioritized. Involving both managers, outside experts, as well as customers or other objective parties is important to producing useful and valid outputs in this step. You may want to create a template along the following lines:

SWOT			SCORE		
Internal Strengths	1	2	3	4	5
a.					
b.					
c.					
d.					
Internal Weaknesses	1	2	3	4	5
a.					
b.					
c.					

Table 11.1 A SWOT Template

Unfortunately, this is where most managers often stop, believing that the ranking itself is the analytical process of the SWOT analysis. However, strategies for competitive advantage still have to be developed, and this may require further work to identify clearly the causal factors leading to particular strengths or weaknesses of the organization.

Step 3: Identify Strategic Fit and Develop a Strategy to Improve Matches

The next step is to identify the company's strategies and strategic fit in light of its internal capabilities and external environment. The resulting fit or misfit should indicate the degree of strategic change the company must make.

In a general sense, you should attempt to develop and recommend strategies that convert important weaknesses into strengths and important threats into opportunities. Finding new markets for a firm's products or services is often a useful conversion strategy. Conversion strategies often require the investment of additional resources, whether in the form of plant, property, equipment, funds, or human.

You should also consider strategies that minimize those weaknesses or avoid the threats that cannot be converted. One strategy is to become a niche player within the larger industry. Another strategy is to reposition the company's products or services.

Four scenarios will become evident as you fill in the quadrants in Figure 11.2 Part B—these will help to determine the existing strategic fit and develop effective strategies to respond to forecasted environmental issues.

To properly determine the strategic fit, try to visualize the company's performance in the future. What will it be if no changes are made to its strategy and its internal and external environments do not change? Also evaluate alternative strategies to find one that provides a competitive advantage for the company. However, while no strategy may become evident that produces a competitive advantage, a SWOT analysis, at a minimum, will help a company to evaluate current and alternative strategies.

Quadrant 1: Internal Strengths Matched with External Opportunities

This is the ideal as it represents the tightest fit between the company's resources and its external competitive opportunities. The strategy would be to protect internal strengths by either finding the combination of resources needed to achieve competitive advantage or augmenting resources to enhance competitive advantage. Explore opportunities to leverage strengths to bolster weaknesses in other areas (most notably those in Quadrant 2).

Quadrant 2: Internal Weaknesses Relative to External Opportunities

The strategy in this quadrant is to choose the optimal trade-off between investing to turn the weaknesses into strengths, outsourcing a weakness where the company does not have a competitive advantage, or allowing rivals to address this particular area.

Quadrant 3: Internal Strengths Matched with External Threats

A strategic option here could be to transform external threats into opportunities by changing, altering, or reconfiguring company resources. Alternatively, choose to maintain a defensive strategy in order to focus on more promising opportunities in other quadrants.

Quadrant 4: Internal Weaknesses Relative to External Threats

This quadrant needs to be carefully addressed and monitored. If the company's survival is at stake as a result of the issues in this quadrant, a proactive strategy may be the only option. If the strategic issues are secondary, a possible option may be to divest in order to focus on other more promising opportunities in other quadrants. It is important, however, to avoid rushing an issue out of this quadrant. Rather, consider the potential it has to provide a significant strategic option to the company or to support more profitable activities in other quadrants. Blind spot analysis to reduce any cultural or thinking biases may be a useful technique for this quadrant.

This step would look like Table 11.2.

Once a strategy is decided on, constantly monitor and analyze current strategies and devise new ones to address developing issues. Consider this approach as a sweep over the environmental radar screen to monitor the movement of identified blips and to benefit from the early warning capabilities afforded by the SWOT technique.

TABLE 11.2 The SWOT Matrix

External	Internal Strengths	Weaknesses
Opportunities	**SO Strategies:** Strategies that leverage internal strengths matched with external opportunities	**WO Strategies:** Strategies that leverage external opportunities to overcome or minimize internal weaknesses
Threats	**ST Strategies:** Strategies that leverage your internal strengths to avoid external threats	**WT Strategies:** Strategies that minimize your internal weaknesses and avoid external threats

Remember, a separate SWOT analysis is required for each business, product, service, or market. One SWOT analysis cannot be all things to all issues. These analyses should be conducted regularly to address the dynamic environment in which we all operate.

Here are three guidance points to keep in mind when undertaking a SWOT analysis:

- Extremely long lists indicate that the screening criteria used to separate information from the strategic issues is too broad.
- The absence of weighting factors indicates a lack of prioritization.
- Short and ambiguously phrased descriptions within each SWOT factor can indicate that the strategic implications have not been considered.

Cannondale Bicycle Corporation

Headquartered in Bethel, Connecticut, Cannondale Bicycle Corporation (Cannondale) designs, develops, and produces bicycles at its factory in Bedford, Pennsylvania. The company operates subsidiaries in Holland, Japan, and Australia and is owned by Pegasus Partners II, L.P., a private equity investment firm based in Greenwich, Connecticut. Its mission is to create innovative, quality products that inspire cyclists around the world. Even though it is helped by its three plus decade track record, Cannondale faces an intense and dynamic global industry environment. The following SWOT analysis presents an integrative view of how its external environment combines with its resources and capabilities (the internal factors) to provide for actionable strategies that can assist the company to achieve its mission.

TABLE 11.3 SWOT Matrix for Cannondale Bicycle Corporation

STRENGTHS (S)	WEAKNESSES (W)
1. Brand recognition	1. Mixed results in diversification efforts
2. Full-line provider across entire value chain	2. High cost of engineering and design talent
3. Scope of retail channels (high-end bike shops)	3. Less experience with carbon frame production
4. Design and engineering prowess	4. Component range low in market share
5. Commitment and dedication of employees	5. Lack of recognition in apparel markets

TABLE 11.3 SWOT Matrix for Cannondale Bicycle Corporation

OPPORTUNITIES (O)	SO Strategies	WO Strategies
1. Co-production of carbon frames in Asia 2. Competitive road and mountain bike teams on three continents seek sponsors 3. Consolidation in industry favors full-line operators and wide retail availability 4. Unique designs being favored 5. Expansion into cycling-related apparel where demand is rising	1. Partner with TopKey for carbon frame production (S2, S4, O1, O3) 2. Inexpensively acquire Asian shoe producer (S1, S3, O3, O5) 3. Use forward contracts and hedging for carbon fiber supply (S2, O1) 4. Leverage Sugoi into carbon fiber shoes, jerseys, and bibs (S1, S3, S5, O4, O5)	1. Tap into waiting sources of investor capital (W1, W3, W5, O3, O5) 2. Expand retail partner network in Asia (W5, O2, O3) 3. Sponsor new Asian professional continental team (W5, O2, O5)
THREATS (T)	ST Strategies	WT Strategies
1. Professional cycling under siege 2. Carbon fiber shortages, high cost of supply 3. Boutique shops attacking high end of market 4. Key new components (drive-train) may require design rethinks 5. Large investments being made into commodity-end (mass market) of business	1. Sponsor club teams in key regions (T1, T5, S1, S5) 2. Rapid prototype components based on relationships developed in testing process (S2, S4, S5, T3, T4) 3. Enhance relationships with full range component suppliers such as Shimano, SRAM, and Campagnolo (S2, S4, T4, T5)	1. Emphasize aluminum frames and components (W2, W3, T2, T4) 2. Divest certain component design and production facilities (W1, W4, T3, T4) 3. Restructure distribution locations to more quickly supply high demand regions (W5, T3, T5)

Note: The numbers following each strategy reflect the interrelationship between identified factors in the development of a particular strategy.

12

Value Chain Analysis

Description and Purpose

Value chain analysis (VCA) is a used to identify a company's potential sources of economic advantage and to achieve an optimal allocation of resources. This is done by reviewing its internal core competencies in light of its external environment. A company's value chain is part of a larger industry value system that includes the value creating activities of all of the industry participants—from raw materials suppliers through to the final consumer. VCA separates the company's processes into strategically relevant value creating activities. This analysis provides rich insights into industry profit and assists to identify strategies needed to generate competitive advantage.

The unique strength of VCA is that it can be used to help companies bridge the strategic gaps between their capabilities and opportunities and threats in their competitive environments. Hence, the two main purposes of VCA are to identify opportunities to secure cost advantages and create product/service attribute differentiation.

The goal of VCA is to help identify strategies that allow your organization to create customer value in excess of the costs of delivering that value—the source of a company's profit. Cost advantages can be achieved by reconfiguring the entire value chain to lessen costs or by lessening the costs of any of the key activities along the chain.

Likewise, differentiation can be achieved through value chain recon-figuration or by delivering innovative ways of generating higher value from a particular activity.

Michael Porter popularized the value chain concept in his 1985 book, *Competitive Advantage* (see Figure 12.1).

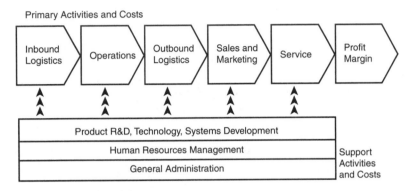

Figure 12.1   The value chain

Adapted from M. Porter, *Competitive Advantage* (New York: The Free Press, 1985).

Porter classifies all of these activities into two main categories:

1. Primary activities
   - **Inbound logistics.** Activities such as inventory warehousing and handling
   - **Operations.** Transformation of inputs into the final product or service
   - **Outbound logistics.** Distribution-oriented activities
   - **Marketing and sales.** Marketing communications, pricing, and channel management
   - **Service.** Post-sale support activities

2. Support activities
   - **Technology development.** Engineering, R&D, and infor-mation technology
   - **Human resource development.** Hiring, incentive sys-tems, motivation, training, promotion, and labor relations

- **Company infrastructure.** Administrative support activities such as accounting, legal, planning, and all forms of stakeholder relations (government and public affairs, community investment, and investor relations)

The price charged to the company's customers, less the costs of all of these activities, determines the company's profit. Obviously, you should be looking to see if your organization is deriving its highest potential margin from the activities it chooses to participate in.

All of the suppliers of the company's inputs as well as forward channel purchasers of the company's products or services will also have their own value chains composed of their primary and support activities. Collectively, all of these value chains comprise the industry value system shown in Figure 12.2.

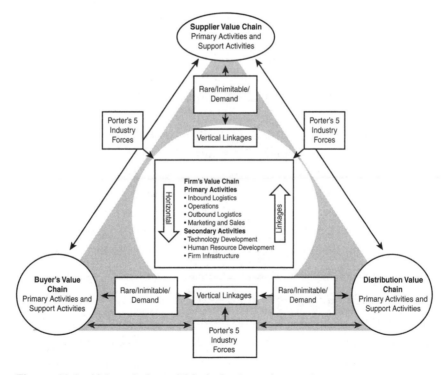

Figure 12.2   Value chains within industry value systems

The totality of activities in the industry's entire value system determines the total customer value created. It is the customers, in deciding the prices they are willing to pay for the products/services produced by the industry, who ultimately determine the margins earned by all of the participants in the industry value system. The share of industry profit earned by each participant is determined by Porter's Five Forces, which shape the industry's structure (see Chapter 6).

VCA is used to determine the current power of the company and suggest how it can increase that power to gain a higher share of industry profit. The following list ranks various types of value chain links in order of their increasing capability to generate competitive advantage:

- **Separate individual activities within the company's value chain.** For example, being an industry leader in inbound logistics
- **Interlinked primary activities in the company's value chain.** For example, increasing quality inspection, which reduces rework, scrap, and customer returns and increases customer value
- **Interlinked secondary activities in the company's value chain.** For example, an organizational structure that fosters learning in all of the relevant activity areas of the company
- **Vertical links within the industry value system.** For example, developing close relationships with suppliers and customers to co-develop low cost or differentiated strategies for mutual but usually disproportionate benefit that is dependent on each party's bargaining strength in the larger value system

VCA will pinpoint opportunities to radically reconfigure industry value systems by eliminating or bypassing entire value chains or major activities within an industry's value system. A well-known example of this is Amazon.com's innovative use of technology and relationship management to bypass the traditional book retailer channel through developing close ties with publishing houses and selling solely over the Internet.

There are also many different secondary applications or subsets of VCA used in the pursuit of competitive strategy. These include

- **Competitor analysis.** Analyzing competitors' cost structures, business models, and sources of differentiation are intrinsic to crafting strategy.

- **Customer value analysis.** Incorporating the common thread of customer value creating activities into the strategy formulation process provides insight that keeps the analysis relevant to this lowest common denominator of profit.

- **Strategic cost management.** Expanding cost management from the traditional approaches of universal cost containment and reduction across the company (to incorporate the unique cost drivers for each value activity) allows for better management of costs. For example, VCA allows the company to identify and then exploit vertical links with suppliers and customers.

- **Integration.** VCA helps companies invest wisely in vertical or horizontal integration strategies or, conversely, to divest, by understanding the impact of the company's value chain and its strategic position in the industry's value system.

- **Supply chain management.** Determining the bargaining power of suppliers as well as recognizing their position in the same industry value system potentially generates opportunities for mutually beneficial co-operation.

- **Strategic outsourcing.** This requires knowledge of the core competencies that can be provided by VCA. With a grasp of the company's core competencies and the relative importance of various activities in the value chain, strategic outsourcing decisions can be made that reduce costs or improve differentiation and flexibility without harming the company's competitive advantage.

- **Acquisition, mergers, alliances, or joint ventures.** Synergy or strategic fit can be advantageously framed by VCA. Target companies can be selected on the basis of how the acquisition would enhance the company's strength in the industry's value system.

- **Organizational structure.** Drawing the boundaries of organizational units based on discrete value creating activities and the vertical links of the value chain will put the company more in tune with the sources of its competitive advantage.

Porter recommended VCA to encourage companies to exploit the often ignored potential vertical synergies that exist between a company's business units and other participants in the industry value system. The logic of VCA is that most sources of competitive advantage lie in these (often intangible) synergies.

Strengths

From the company's perspective, VCA is a useful tool for understanding its strengths and weaknesses. From an industry perspective, VCA provides a helpful understanding of its competitive position relative to key customers and suppliers. VCA also provides a good understanding of the nature and sustainability of the company's resources and capabilities and what new resources and capabilities it might require to be competitive in the future. For those individuals who are doing a SWOT analysis as part of their insight development process, the VCA will provide a much better real-world sense of what is really a strength or a weakness (see Chapter 11).

VCA encourages the company to comprehensively review all of the value creating activities that deliver value to the customer. It is also more inclusive of the complex economic cost drivers that affect customer value, such as structural drivers (for example, scale, scope, experience, technology, complexity) and executional drivers (for example, management style, total quality management, plant layout, capacity utilization, product configuration, vertical links with suppliers, and customers).

As we can see, VCA builds a holistic cost/value analysis that more closely models economic reality because of its external customer and industry focus. It can help to generate ideas about new revenue-side and cost-based pathways for adding value.

If your company has adopted activity-based accounting (ABA), the process of VCA will be easier, as ABA eliminates many of the distortions of traditional management accounting. In fact, activity-based management (ABM) shares many similarities with VCA. VCA works particularly well for those companies that already employ activity-based costing (ABC), competitor benchmarking, Six Sigma, or similar management accounting or statistical control processes. Combined and updated with these sources of data, VCA can generate some of the best, empirically-based insights for understanding exactly where margin is augmented or deteriorated.

Weaknesses

Despite the strengths of VCA, its usefulness is being challenged by the radical changes that information technologies have wrought. A growing school of management thought asserts that traditional value chains oriented around vertical linkages cannot constantly reinvent value at the speed required for successful strategy.

Traditional VCA was developed for understanding physical assets and flows. It may not be as appropriate to employ for competition based around intellectual assets and/or services. Having stated that, there are newer conceptual developments happening that increasingly allow for modification of the traditional VCA for evolving or newer modes of competitiveness including value net analysis, value grid analysis, value migration, value constellation analysis, value stream mapping, value shop analysis, service value chains, and so on.

Managing value chains in an information communication and technology environment requires the inclusion of economic realities that are not explicitly addressed by Porter's VCA model. VCA treats information as a supporting element in the company's strategy—at best it is only part of a secondary activity. Recently evolved models such as the virtual value chain and value web management treat information as a separate and distinct value creating factor that must be managed separately but together with the enduring physical value chain.

Porter has also been criticized for being too simplistic because many of his qualitative prescriptions are difficult to implement quantitatively—the most prominent shortcoming being that they require significant amounts of resources. Effective VCA requires a large investment in benchmarking, customer research, competitive analysis, and industry structure analysis, often using data that is either not freely or easily available. Conducting VCA might be straightforward in theory, but it is relatively difficult and time-consuming to apply for maximum, valid effect.

Further, most of a company's internal accounting data are incompatible with the analytical dimensions of VCA for several reasons. Traditional management accounting systems rarely, if ever

- Collect data around value creating activities. Instead, they collect data around product/service and period costs.
- Collect period costs by product or service, making it difficult to accurately assign overhead costs to value creating processes.
- Collect data around cost drivers. Departmental budgets will rarely be an accurate source for determining the actual cost of value creating activities.
- Enable transfer prices and arbitrary cost allocation of traditional management accounting systems to appropriately encompass the synergies created by horizontal links in the company's value chain or the vertical links in the industry's value system.

How to Do It

Conducting a successful VCA requires judgment, attention to detail, competitive knowledge, and quantitative analysis. Understanding the company's industry structure and, more importantly, aligning this knowledge with the company's capabilities, are intrinsic to crafting successful strategies.

The VCA process begins with an internal analysis of the company's value chain followed by an external competitive analysis of the industry value system. It concludes by integrating these two analyses to identify/create a strategy that can potentially sustain competitive advantage.

Step 1: Define the Company's Strategic Business Units

The first level of review draws boundaries around the various segments of the business. This is necessary because the different segments of the business will have different sources of competitive advantage that require different strategies.

Usually, the company's organizational structure or accounting system will not classify business units in a manner consistent with business unit operations. You must frequently divorce yourself from the usual classifications, such as departments and functions or cost, revenue, and investment centers. This leaves you with two conflicting criteria to define your business units either by

- Autonomy (where managerial decisions about one business unit will have little or no impact on the other business unit)
- Their ability to support VCA (shared links within the company and between value chains in the value system)

Where the two criteria conflict, it is probably best to choose the latter, as a key purpose of VCA is to leverage shared linkages—a high potential source of competitive advantage.

Step 2: Identify the Company's Critical Value Creating Activities

For companies that haven't adopted ABA, Porter offers several distinctions that define value creating activities. They are those that

- Have different economic structures
- Contribute to a large or growing percentage of total costs
- Contribute to or stand a high probability of contributing to product/service differentiation

Tables 12.1 and 12.2 might provide suggestions of what to look for.

TABLE 12.1 Assessing the Primary Activities in the Value Chain

Inbound Logistics

- What type of inventory control system is there? How well does it work?
- How are raw materials handled and warehoused? How efficiently?
- How is material received? From whom? Where is it acquired?

Operations

- Areas to be reviewed include machining, testing, packaging, equipment maintenance, and so on with questions such as:
- How productive and efficient is our equipment compared to our competitors?
- What type of plant layout is used? How efficient is it?
- Are production control systems in place to control quality and reduce costs? How efficient and effective are they in doing so?
- Are we using the appropriate level of automation in our production processes? Are employees properly trained to use it? Is it upgradeable?

Outbound Logistics

- Are finished products warehoused efficiently? How much waste do we experience?
- How do we manage order processing? What percent is automated?
- Are finished products efficiently delivered to customers? Are our delivery operations appropriate and effective?
- Are finished products delivered in a timely fashion to customers?

TABLE 12.1 Assessing the Primary Activities in the Value Chain

Marketing and Sales

- Is marketing research effectively used to identify customer segments and needs?
- Are sales promotions and advertising innovative?
- Have alternative distribution channels been evaluated? How do we select and manage our distribution channels?
- How competent is the sales force operation? Is its level of motivation as high as it can be? Are they perceived to be helpful to customers, both current and potential?
- Does our organization present an image of quality to our customers? Does our organization have a favorable reputation?
- How brand-loyal are our customers and our competitors' customers? Does our customer brand loyalty need improvement?
- Do we dominate the various market segments we're in?

Customer Service

- How well do we solicit customer input for product improvements?
- How promptly and effectively are customer complaints handled?
- Are our product warranty and guarantee policies appropriate?
- How effectively do we train employees in customer education and service issues?
- How well do we handle installation?
- How well do we provide replacement parts and repair services?

Adapted from Mary K. Coulter, *Strategic Management in Action*, Second Edition (Upper Saddle River, NJ: Prentice-Hall, Inc, 2002: 133).

TABLE 12.2 Assessing the Support Activities in the Value Chain

Procurement

- Have we developed alternative suppliers for all our needed resources?
- Are resources procured in a timely fashion? At lowest possible cost? At acceptable quality levels?
- Is purchasing centered or decentralized? What would be most effective and efficient?
- How efficient and effective are our procedures for procuring large capital expenditure resources such as plants, machinery, and buildings?
- Are criteria in place for deciding on lease versus purchase decisions?
- Have we established sound long-term relationships with reliable suppliers?

Technological Development

- How successful have our research and development activities been in product and process innovations?
- Is the relationship between R&D employees and other departments strong and reliable? Do they work seamlessly with one another?
- Have technology development activities been able to meet criteria deadlines?
- What is the quality of our organization's laboratories and other research facilities?
- Have we taken advantage of office automation and telecommunications technologies?
- Does our organizational culture encourage creativity and innovation?

TABLE 12.2 Assessing the Support Activities in the Value Chain

Human Resource Management

- How effective are our procedures for recruiting, selecting, orienting, and training employees?
- Are there appropriate employee promotion policies in place, and are they used effectively?
- How appropriate are reward systems for motivating and challenging employees?
- Do we have a work environment that minimizes absenteeism and keeps turnover at reasonable levels?
- Are union-organization relations (if applicable) acceptable?
- Do managers and technical personnel actively participate in professional organizations?
- Are employees empowered with decision-making capabilities as required?
- Are levels of employee motivation, job commitment, and job satisfaction acceptable?

Company Infrastructure

- Is our organization able to identify potential external opportunities or threats? Do we have an early warning system?
- Does our strategic planning system facilitate and enhance the accomplishment of organizational goals?
- Can we obtain relatively low cost funds for capital expenditures and working capital?
- Does our information system support strategic and operational decision making? Does our information system provide timely and accurate information on general environmental trends and competitive conditions?
- Do our communication processes facilitate fast and transparent message sharing with key stakeholders, both inside and outside the organization?
- Do we have good relationships with all our stakeholders including public policy makers, interest groups, and so on?
- Do we have a good public image of being a responsible corporate citizen?

Adapted from Mary K. Coulter, *Strategic Management in Action*, Second Edition (Upper Saddle River, NJ: Prentice-Hall, Inc, 2002: 134).

Step 3: Conduct Internal Cost Analysis

An internal cost analysis is composed of the following:

- **Assign costs to each critical value creating activity identified in Step 2.** It is recommended that a full costing or a product life cycle costing approach be used that incorporates full capacity utilization.

- **Find the cost drivers for each critical value creating activity that is driven by more than one major cost category.** Structural cost drivers are long-term in nature and affect the economic cost structure of the company's products and services. (Consider scale, scope, learning curves, technology, and complexity.) Executional cost drivers are more operational in nature. (Consider management style, total quality management, plant layout, capacity utilization, product configuration, and vertical links with suppliers and customers.)

- **Diagnose the company's current strategy for areas of potential low cost advantage.** Search for horizontal links in the company's value chain in the form of interlinked value creating activities that reduce costs by virtue of their symbiosis. This is the time to explore opportunities for cost management. It is important to focus externally to compare the company's cost structure to its competition through benchmarking and associated practice comparisons. Business process design and re-engineering approaches can then be utilized to secure any potential low cost advantages.

Step 4: Conduct Internal Differentiation Analysis

Similar to the internal cost analysis, the internal differentiation analysis starts with identifying the company's value creating activities and cost drivers. Next, you link your customer and competitive knowledge with the appropriate strategy through the following steps:

- **Conduct customer research to determine a precise definition of customer value**. Helpful ways to secure this knowledge are to engage in a dialog with customers and analyze the customer's own value chain to gain insights into how your company's products and services may provide additional value to them.

- **Identify strategies that can differentiate your company's products and services**. This could include product or service attributes, channel management, customer support, pre- and post-sale support, branding, and price. Based on the company's core competencies, choose the best differentiation strategy to achieve competitive advantage by offering a product or service that is rare, in demand, and difficult for competitors to imitate.

Step 5: Map Industry Profit Pool

a. Define the Parameters of the Industry Profit Pool

The parameters of the industry profit pool are dependent on the value chain processes that affect the company's current and future ability to earn profit. It is helpful to assume the perspective of the company, competitors, and customers. Include all of the relevant value creating activities, starting with the purchase of raw material inputs and ending with the total cost of ownership to the final consumer. Note, the final consumer may not be your company's purchasers.

b. Estimate the Total Size of the Industry Profit Pool

Employ several different estimation methodologies to gauge the total size of the profit pool, for example, by companies, products, channels, or regions. Usually, accounting profit will suffice for profit. However, when mapping the profit pool of an industry with international participants, economic value added (EVA) can be used because it eliminates many of the distortions caused by various national generally accepted accounting principles (GAAP) regimes. Some sources of information for these estimates are analyst reports, financial statements, security commission reports, and by engaging industry experts.

c. Estimate the Distribution of the Profit Pool

A good starting point is to use your company's profit structure by activity (that is Steps 1 through 4) in the external analysis of rival companies in the industry. Following are a few general rules for this stage.

- Use your knowledge of the underlying economics of your own company to outline each activity's profit. Take care to segregate allocated costs. This information can be used as a relative gauge to estimate the activity profits of rival companies in the industry.

- Sources of competitive information include financial statements, analyst reports, security exchange commission filings, trade journals, the business press, industry associations, and government regulators.

- A helpful hint is to use the market value or replacement costs of assets that support value creating activities and the full costing approach under full capacity for costing the same value creating activities.

- Use the 80/20 rule—this suggests that 20 percent of the industry's companies will generate 80 percent of the industry profit; therefore, concentrate on the largest companies first.

- The level of analytical detail will depend on the degree of vertical integration present in the industry. Start with the focused companies first and then estimate the relevant activity profits of diversified companies by adjusting your knowledge of your own company's economics and that of the focused companies in the industry. Next, include the smaller companies (the 80 percent responsible for 20 percent of industry profit), based on sampling.

- For accuracy, total the activity profits determined in this step and compare them to the total industry profit pool determined in Step 5, Part b earlier. If the two estimates are wildly divergent, change the assumptions and tweak the methodology through iteration until the two estimates are reasonably similar.

A graphical representation of an industry profit pool should look similar to Figure 12.3. The results could be surprising in that the activities that command the largest industry revenue share may receive a disproportionately low share of industry profits.

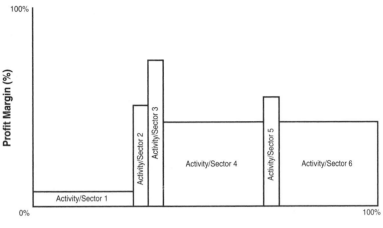

Figure 12.3 Stylistic industry profit pool graphic

Step 6: Vertical Linkage Analysis

The opportunities to achieve cost and differentiation advantages within the company's value chain were reviewed in Steps 1 to 4. Step 5 allowed you to determine whether the company is strategically positioned in the shallow or deep end of the industry's profit pool. Vertical linkage analysis allows you to seek out opportunities to exploit the most important sources of competitive advantage in the industry's value system. You can combine your intimate knowledge of the company's economic structure, customer value, and external competitive analysis to determine how to reposition the company into the deep end of the industry profit pool—and keep it there.

The methodology to accomplish this is the crux of vertical linkage analysis. This is also the most difficult stage because many of the vertical linkages in the industry's value chain are less tangible and extremely difficult to discover. Nevertheless, it is because of this difficulty that VCA often offers a direct route to competitive advantage. The methodology consists of the following stages:

1. Use Porter's Five Forces model to determine the industry's economic structure (see Chapter 6).

2. Determine the cost drivers and core competencies driving the low cost or differentiation for each of the value creating activities of competitors.

3. Evaluate the company's core competencies—those capabilities, skills, and technologies that create low cost or differentiated customer value. Usually, core competencies are acquired through collective learning and relationships. Identify any opportunities to surpass competing customer offerings by securing missing competencies or supplementing existing competencies needed to successfully craft, maintain, and strengthen a low cost or differentiation strategy.

4. Based on the relative bargaining strength of other value chains in the value system, determine opportunities to acquire or strengthen the required competencies through vertical linkages with suppliers, channels, or buyers in the value system.

5. Avoid the temptation to settle for a mixed strategy—part differentiation and part low cost. This is the easy way, but it will not generate competitive advantage for the average company; rather, it will leave a company wading aimlessly in the shallow end of the industry profit pool. A growing body of academic work, validated by practice, asserts that crafting successful strategy is valuable because of the often painful trade-offs it forces executives to make. Mixed strategies offer a chance of success only for companies that are pushing the frontier of production possibilities or for those that have a truly integrated global strategy.

6. Identify any potential opportunities for competitive advantage in the vertical linkages between the company's value chain and the value chains of suppliers, channels, and customers. By co-opting or cooperating with other value chains in the industry's value system, the company can often craft a low cost or differentiated strategy that is impossible for competitors to replicate. Complex and less or intangible vertical linkages offer the most impenetrable combinations of rarity, demand, and inimitability—the triad underlying competitive advantage.

Step 7: Iteration

Repeat Steps 1 to 6 periodically by making VCA a central component of your company's competitive intelligence and strategy development system in order to proactively manage evolutionary and revolutionary industry change.

Case Study

IKEA

Sweden's IKEA Furniture presents an excellent example of how companies can use the concept of VCA to reconfigure industry value chains to their benefit. VCA played a prominent role in IKEA's growth from a small, domestic, mail-order furniture company into a multinational chain of more than 260 stores in more than 37 countries with 2007 revenues of 20.6 million euros and a global customer base of over 580 million. More importantly, IKEA has profitably managed this growth, as witnessed by an estimated 10 percent profit margin in a notoriously low margin discount furniture industry. An initial analysis of IKEA's business model would suggest that it was able to achieve this through efficient and effective management of its internal value chain: low cost components, efficient warehousing, and customer self-service have allowed it to offer discounts 25–50 percent below its competitors. IKEA's true source of success goes much deeper than this, however, and can be shown by its skillful management of the industry value system.

IKEA has successfully reconfigured its industry value system by redefining almost every aspect of its industry through leveraging vertical links in its value system. It used many of the individual value chains within its industry value system to increase its power in the furniture industry.

Supplier's Value Chain

IKEA has 38 factories in eleven countries, mostly in Eastern and Central Europe, and its operations cover every step of production—forestry, sawmilling, board manufacture, and furniture production.

However, a major source of IKEA's low cost is derived from extensive outsourcing. IKEA works closely with its suppliers in a cooperative relationship to mutually exploit synergies. Forty-five IKEA trading offices in 31 countries evaluate 1,350 suppliers in 50 countries for low cost and high quality. Furniture designers in the home office in Almhut, Sweden, work two to three years ahead of the current product life cycle to determine which supplier will provide parts. Once accepted, IKEA provides suppliers with economies of scale associated with global markets, technical assistance, and leased equipment. Suppliers also receive quality advice from IKEA engineers and have access to a computer database to assist in sourcing raw materials and matching suppliers with each other from the business service department.

Distribution Value Chain

To manage and support its global network of suppliers, IKEA operates 31 distribution centers in 16 countries. These centers supply goods to IKEA stores and ensure that the route from supplier to customer is as direct, cost-effective, and environmentally friendly as possible. Efficient distribution plays a key role in maintaining low prices.

Direct links from every cash register in every store to these warehouses are an integral part of the cost reduction strategy, as they support lean inventory management. They also support customer value by allowing IKEA to tightly integrate supply with demand.

Customer Value Chain

The cornerstone of IKEA's strategy is to convince customers that it is in their best interests to assume more responsibility in creating value by performing more activities in the industry value system themselves—choosing, ordering, delivering, and assembling products in exchange for low cost, high quality products. To encourage this radical redesign of the value system, IKEA employs its core competence—its knowledge of how to make these activities easy, enjoyable, and valuable for its customers:

- IKEA produces more than 191 million catalogs per annum in 56 editions and 27 languages for 34 countries/territories. Each catalog carries only 30 to 40 percent of the entire 9,500-item product line, transcending the traditional role of the catalog as a simple ordering tool. The IKEA website also attracted 450 million visits during the last 12 months worldwide. In effect, the catalog and the Internet function as a role-playing guide, essentially explaining to the customer what is expected of them in exchange for exceptional discounts on high quality furniture at their local IKEA stores.

- Shopping at IKEA is designed to be fun. IKEA provides shoppers with many value creating amenities that increase the value of the shopping experience—strollers, supervised daycare, playgrounds, cafes, restaurants, and wheelchairs for the disabled, some of which are free of charge.

- Shopping at IKEA is easy, quick, and productive. The company provides several tools to assist customers in creating their own value in partnership with IKEA. Items such as catalogs, tape measures, pens, and paper are provided free of charge. Design ideas are created through IKEA's store displays. Each item in these displays is tagged with only the necessary details—product name, price, available dimensions, materials, color, care instructions, and order and pickup location. If the chosen merchandise doesn't fit in the customer's vehicle, IKEA will lend a roof rack.

VCA has allowed IKEA to offer its customers what no one else has—a large selection of high quality furniture at low cost. This combination dismisses many of the traditional trade-offs long held sacrosanct in the furniture industry. By leveraging the vertical linkages in its value system, IKEA's strategy is rare, in demand, and difficult to imitate—it is well entrenched at the deep end of the industry profit pool.

Case study adapted from R. Normann and R. Ramirez, "From Value Chain to Value Constellation: Designing Interactive Strategy," *Harvard Business Review* 71(4), 1993: 65–77.

INDEX

A

ABA (activity-based accounting), 204
ABM (activity-based management), 205
acceptance, lack of, for STEEP analysis, 174
accounting equation in FRSA, 67-68
accounting methods, effect on income statements, 72
accounting periods, defined, 68
accounts receivable ratios in FRSA, 75-76
accounts receivable to sales ratio, 75
accounts receivable turnover ratio, 76
accuracy of collected data, 19
acid test ratio, 79
acquisitions, value chain analysis and, 203
activity-based accounting (ABA), 204
activity-based management (ABM), 205
advocacy issues, 122
airline industry case study (Five Forces Industry Analysis), 105-107
alliances, value chain analysis and, 203
Almanac of Business and Industrial Financial Ratios, 86
Alon and Martin framework (political risk analysis), 140-146
ambiguity, 13
analysis
    challenges addressed by, 12-13
    cognitive biases in, 22-23
    competencies for conducting, 23

    data collection, role in, 19-20
    defined, 6, 18-19
    as element of strategic thinking, 23
    generic process to, 19
    purpose of, 8
    reasons for lack of, 15-17
    reasons for need for, 8-11
    results of, 8
    scientific method comparison, 17
    warnings concerning, 20-21
analysis techniques. *See* BCG matrix; competitor analysis; Five Forces Industry Analysis; FRSA; issue analysis; political risk analysis; scenario analysis; STEEP analysis; SWOT analysis; value chain analysis
analytical dynamics, including in BCG matrix, 43-44
Andrews, Ken, 184
Annual Statement Studies: Industry Default Probabilities and Cash Flow Measures, 2005–2006, 87
assessment in Five Forces Industry Analysis, 103-104
asset turnover ratios in FRSA, 76
assets, defined, 67
assumptions of competitors, identifying, 57, 64
attacking groups (issue response pattern), 126
attention groups (issue expansion map), 120
attentive public (issue expansion map), 120

average collection periods, 75
average inventory investment
  period, 74

B

balance sheets, defined, 68
bargaining (issue response
  pattern), 126
bargaining power
  of buyers, 98
  of suppliers, 97
Baser Foods case study (political risk
  analysis), 146-149
BCG matrix
  case study, 45-47
  experience curve theory and, 30-31
  product life cycle and, 31-32
  purpose of, 29-30
  quadrants in, 32-33, 35
  steps in, 38-44
  strengths of, 35-36
  weaknesses of, 36-38
biases in analysis, 22-23
blurring (issue response pattern), 126
Boston Consulting Group. See
  BCG matrix
brands (STEEP analysis case study),
  179-181
broadband cable TV industry case
  study, 45-47
business management
  defined, 3
  requirements of, 18
business units. See SBUs (strategic
  business units)
buyers, bargaining power of, 98

C

Cannondale Bicycle Corporation
  case study (SWOT analysis),
  196-197
capabilities of competitors,
  determining, 56, 64
capital market analysis ratios in
  FRSA, 82
capitulation (issue response
  pattern), 126
case studies
  BCG matrix, 45-47
  competitor analysis, 61-65

Five Forces Industry Analysis,
  105-109
FRSA, 91-93
issue analysis, 128-129
political risk analysis, 146-147, 149
scenario analysis, 163-167
STEEP analysis, 179-181
SWOT analysis, 196-197
value chain analysis, 217-219
"cash cows" (in BCG matrix), 33
cash flow, 70
cessation (issue response
  pattern), 127
cognitive biases in analysis, 22-23
collecting data. See data collection
commitment, escalating, 22
comparison grids, 58
comparison of ratios in FRSA, 84
  industrial comparisons, 84, 89
  performance history comparisons,
    89-91
competencies
  for conducting analysis, 23
  defined, 3, 10
competition, intensity of, 99
competitive advantage, defined, 4
Competitive Advantage (Porter), 200
competitive position (in BCG
  matrix), 32
competitor analysis, 45, 203
  with BCG matrix, 36
  case study, 61-65
  purpose of, 49-51
  steps in, 52-60
  strengths of, 51
  weaknesses of, 51-52
competitor comparisons in ratio
  analysis, 69
competitor matrices, constructing
  for BCG matrix, 42
complexity, increasing, 10
computer-generated econometric
  model (scenario analysis), 152
consistency in scenario analysis, 160
consolidated financial statements,
  segmented financial statements
  versus, 89, 91
content analysis, 115
control, illusion of, 22
cross-impact method (scenario
  analysis), 153

current assets, defined, 67
current issues, 120-121
current liabilities, defined, 68
current ratio, 78
current strategy of competitors, 56, 63
customer value analysis, 203

D

data collection
  in Five Forces Industry Analysis, 102
  in political risk analysis, 134-135
  role in analysis, 19-20
debt to assets ratio, 77
debt to equity ratio, 77
decision scenarios in scenario
  analysis, 160
deductive reduction, 154
Dell case study (FRSA), 91-93
Delphi method (scenario
  analysis), 153
Delphi panels, 115
diffusion (issue response
  pattern), 126
diversification scenarios, 155
diversified businesses, effect on
  STEEP analysis, 175
"dogs" (in BCG matrix), 34

E

earnings per share (EPS), 82
economic factors in political risk
  analysis, 143-144
emerging issues, 120-121
entry barriers, role of, 96-97
environment, levels of, 169-170
environmental analysis. See STEEP
  analysis
environmental boundaries,
  establishing (STEEP analysis), 175
EPS (earnings per share), 82
escalating commitment, 22
evaluation in Five Forces Industry
  Analysis, 103-104
events in STEEP analysis,
  defined, 176
experience curve theory, BCG
  matrix and, 30-31
expertise, seeking (political risk
  analysis), 139-140

external environment, SWOT
  analysis, 183, 187
external factors in political risk
  analysis, 143-144
external opportunities
  internal weaknesses relative to, 194
  matching with internal
    strengths, 193
external threats
  internal weaknesses relative to, 194
  matching with internal
    strengths, 194

F

false alarm scenario (scenario
  analysis case study), 164
File 101 DISCLOSURE
  DATABASE, 85
File 519 D&B—Duns Financial
  Records Plus® (DFR), 86
financial ratio and statement
  analysis. See FRSA
financial statement analysis, defined,
  67. See also FRSA
financial statements
  components of, 68-69
  consolidated versus segmented
    financial statements, 89, 91
Five Forces Industry Analysis
  buyers, bargaining power of, 98
  case study, 105-109
  competition, intensity of, 99
  entry barriers, role of, 96-97
  market displacement, threat of,
    98-99
  objective of, 95-96
  steps in, 102-105
  strengths of, 100
  suppliers, bargaining power of, 97
  weaknesses of, 101
fixed assets, defined, 68
fixed charge coverage, 77
forecasting
  future direction of issues in STEEP
    analysis, 178-179
  in issue analysis, 115-121
formation stage (issue life cycle), 116
formatting competitive analysis
  results, 58-60

fractionation of trends, 177
FRSA (financial ratio and statement analysis), 67
    accounting equation in, 67-68
    accounts receivable ratios in, 75-76
    asset turnover ratios in, 76
    capital market analysis ratios in, 82
    case study, 91-93
    financial ratios, list of, 83-84
    financial statements, components of, 68-69
    inventory ratios in, 74-75
    liquidity analysis ratios in, 78-79
    profitability analysis ratios in, 80-81
    ratio comparison in, 84, 89-91
    ratios, assessing appropriateness of, 69-70
    shareholder returns analysis ratios in, 82
    solvency analysis ratios in, 76-78
    steps in, 73
    strengths of, 70
    weaknesses of, 70, 72-73
future goals of competitors, 56, 62
future uncertainty, dealing with, 162

G–H

GE (General Electric), 29
general environment in STEEP analysis, 170
general public (issue expansion map), 120
globalization, 8-9
government regulation scenario (scenario analysis case study), 165
governmental factors in political risk analysis, 141-143
governmental macrorisks, defined, 136
governmental microrisks, defined, 137
grand tours approach (political risk analysis), 139
gross profit margin, 81
"groupthink," 22
growth rate
    plotting on BCG matrix, 40
    of SBUs/SBLs, measuring, 39
Growth/Share portfolio matrix. *See* BCG matrix

I

identification groups (issue expansion map), 120
IKEA case study (value chain analysis), 217-219
illusion of control, 22
imitators, abundance of, 10
impact/probability matrix in scenario analysis case study, 163-167
impacts of trends, 177
implications of STEEP analysis, 179
inaccuracy in STEEP analysis, 174
income statements, defined, 68
inductive reduction, 154
industrial comparisons in FRSA, 84, 89
industry analysis. *See* Five Forces Industry Analysis
industry norms, reliance on, 71-72
industry profit pool, mapping in value chain analysis, 213-214
industry scenarios, 155
industry-wide comparisons in ratio analysis, 70
information, knowledge versus, 9
information collection in Five Forces Industry Analysis, 102
information retrieval, 13
institutionalized issues, 121
intangible assets, 71
Integra Information, 88
integration, value chain analysis and, 203
interest coverage, 78
interest groups, 117
internal cost analysis in value chain analysis, 212
internal differentiation analysis in value chain analysis, 212-213
internal environment, SWOT analysis, 183, 187
internal factors in political risk analysis
    economic factors, 143
    governmental factors, 141-142
    societal factors, 142
internal strengths, matching with external opportunities/threats, 193-194

internal weaknesses, relative to external opportunities/threats, 194
interpretation in STEEP analysis, 174
intuitive method (scenario analysis), 153
inventory ratios in FRSA, 74-75
inventory to sales ratio, 74
issue analysis
  case study, 128-129
  purpose of, 111-113
  steps in, 115-128
  strengths of, 113-114
  weaknesses of, 114
issue assessment in issue analysis, 121-123
issue expansion map, 119-120
issue identification in issue analysis, 115-121
issue impact (assessing issues), 122
issue life cycle
  four-stage progression, 116-117
  seven-stage progression, 118-119
issue timing, 120-121
issues (STEEP analysis)
  forecasting future direction of, 178-179
  relating trends to, 178
issues distance (assessing issues), 121

J–K

joint ventures, value chain analysis and, 203

Key Business Ratios on the Web, 86
knowledge, information versus, 9
knowledge economy, 9-10

L

latent issues, 120
learning function (in experience curve), 30
learning scenarios in scenario analysis, 160
legislative formalization stage (issue life cycle), 117
leverage analysis ratios. *See* solvency analysis ratios in FRSA
liabilities, defined, 68

liquidity analysis ratios in FRSA, 78-79
long-term liabilities, defined, 68

M

macroenvironmental analysis. *See* STEEP analysis
macrorisks, 136-138
magnitude of trends, 177
management choices, effect on financial statements, 72
mapping industry profit pool in value chain analysis, 213-214
market attractiveness (in BCG matrix), 32
market displacement, threat of, 98-99
market growth rate. *See* growth rate
mergers, value chain analysis and, 203
microrisks, 136-138
Minnegasco case study, 128-129
misperceptions of STEEP analysis, 175
mixed scenario method (scenario analysis), 154

N–O

negative impacts of trends, 177
net profit margin, 81
neutral impacts of trends, 177
noncurrent assets, defined, 68

offshoring, defined, 132
old hands approach (political risk analysis), 139-140
operational decisions, defined, 5
opportunities
  defined, 191
  listing in SWOT analysis, 190-191
  ranking in SWOT analysis, 191-192
  strategy development in SWOT analysis, 192-195
organizational structure, value chain analysis and, 203
outsourcing
  offshoring, defined, 132
  strategic outsourcing, 203
overconfidence, 22
oversimplification, 22
owners' equity, defined, 68

P

P/E (price/earnings) ratio, 82
performance history
    comparisons in FRSA, 89-91
    in ratio analysis, 69
    reliance on, 72
PEST analysis. *See* STEEP analysis
pharmaceutical industry case study
    Five Forces Industry Analysis,
        107-109
    scenario analysis, 163-167
plausibility in scenario analysis, 160
PLC (product life cycle), BCG
    matrix and, 31-32
plotting SBUs/SBLs on BCG matrix,
    40-41
political risk, defined, 131
political risk analysis
    Alon and Martin framework, 140-146
    case study, 146-149
    components of, 135-138
    external factors, 143-144
    internal factors, 141-143
    purpose of, 131-132
    qualitative techniques, 138-140
    quantitative techniques, 140-141
    strengths of, 132-134
    weaknesses of, 134-135
politicization stage (issue life
    cycle), 117
Porter, Michael, 49, 95, 200
portfolio matrix. *See* BCG matrix
position statements, defined, 69
positive impacts of trends, 177
PP (public policy). *See* issue analysis
PRA. *See* political risk analysis
price/earnings ratio, 82
primary activities in value chain
    analysis, 200, 208-209
prior hypothesis bias, 22
prioritizing issues, 123
"problem children" (in BCG matrix),
    34-35
product life cycle, BCG matrix and,
    31-32
profitability analysis ratios in FRSA,
    80-81
public environmental intelligence, 111
public issue scenarios, 155
public policy. *See* issue analysis

Q

*QFR: Quarterly Financial Report for
    Manufacturing, Mining and Trade
    Corporations*, 87
qualitative methods
    for political risk analysis, 138-140
    of scenario analysis, 153-154
quantitative methods
    for political risk analysis, 140-141
    of scenario analysis, 152
quantitative models in scenario
    analysis, 160
quick ratio, 79

R

radar charts, 58
ranking SWOT analysis factors,
    191-192
rate of change for trends, 176
ratio analysis, defined, 67. *See also*
    FRSA
ratio comparison in FRSA, 84
    industrial comparisons, 84, 89
    performance history comparisons,
        89-91
ratios, assessing appropriateness of,
    69-70
regulation/litigation stage (issue life
    cycle), 117
relative market share
    plotting on BCG matrix, 40
    of SBUs/SBLs, measuring, 39
reliability of collected data, 19
representativeness bias, 23
research needs, identifying in
    scenario analysis, 160
resistance (issue response
    pattern), 126
response patterns in issue analysis,
    125-128
risk, 131. *See also* political risk
    analysis
ROA (return on assets) ratio, 80
ROE (return on equity) ratio, 80

S

SBLs (strategic business lines)
    assigning strategies to, 42
    measuring growth rate of, 39

measuring relative market share
of, 39
plotting on BCG matrix, 40-41
segmentation of, 38-39
SBUs (strategic business units)
assigning strategies to, 42
defining in value chain analysis, 207
measuring growth rate of, 39
measuring relative market share
of, 39
plotting on BCG matrix, 40-41
segmentation of, 38-39
scale function (in experience
curve), 30
scenario analysis
case study, 163-167
purpose of, 151-152
qualitative methods, 153-154
quantitative methods, 152
scenario types in, 154-155
steps in, 158-160, 162-163
strengths of, 156-157
success factors in, 155
weaknesses of, 157-158
scenario development, 115
scenarios
defined, 151
types of, 154-155
scientific method, analysis
comparison, 17
SCIP (Society of Competitive
Intelligence Professionals), 23
scope of scenario analysis, 159
segmented financial statements,
consolidated financial statements
versus, 89, 91
selective issues, 122
self-regulation scenario (scenario
analysis case study), 165
semi-log graphs, 40
sensitivity scenarios, 154
share momentum graph, 43
shareholder returns analysis ratios in
FRSA, 82
short-term orientation, STEEP
analysis versus, 174
simplification of problems, 22
situation analysis. See SWOT
analysis
societal factors in political risk
analysis, 142-143

societal issues, 121
societal macrorisks, defined, 136
societal microrisks, defined, 137
Society of Competitive Intelligence
Professionals (SCIP), 23
solvency analysis ratios in FRSA,
76-78
specialization function (in
experience curve), 30
speed of change, 10
stakeholders, identifying for scenario
analysis, 159
Standard & Poor's Industry
Surveys, 88
"stars" (in BCG matrix), 33
statement of changes in owner's
equity, defined, 69
statistical techniques for political
risk analysis, 140
STEEP analysis
case study, 179-181
environmental levels in, 169-170
purpose of, 169-171
STEEP scenarios versus, 154
steps in, 175-179
strengths of, 172-173
variables in, 171
weaknesses of, 174-175
STEEP scenarios, STEEP analysis
versus, 154
strategic business lines. See SBLs
strategic business units. See SBUs
strategic cost management, 203
strategic decisions, defined, 5
strategic evaluation, 45
strategic issues, defined, 187
strategic management, defined, 3
strategic outsourcing, 203
strategic planning, defined, 4
strategic thinking, analysis in, 23
strategy development
in Five Forces Industry Analysis,
104-105
management decisions in, 4-5
in SWOT analysis, 192, 194-195
strengths
defined, 190
listing in SWOT analysis, 190-191
ranking in SWOT analysis, 191-192
strategy development in SWOT
analysis, 192, 194-195

suppliers, bargaining power of, 97
supply chain management, 203
support activities in value chain
    analysis, 200, 210-211
survey techniques, 115
sustainable growth rate analysis, 44
SWOT analysis
    case study, 196-197
    purpose of, 183-184, 187-188
    steps in, 190-195
    strengths of, 188-189
    weaknesses of, 189-190

T

tactical decisions, defined, 5
technical issues, 122
termination (issue response
    pattern), 127
threats
    defined, 191
    listing in SWOT analysis, 190-191
    ranking in SWOT analysis, 191-192
    strategy development in SWOT
        analysis, 192-195
time, lack of, 13
Times Interest Earned Ratio, 78
timing (of issues), 120-121
total disclosure scenario (scenario
    analysis case study), 165
trend analysis with BCG matrix, 36
trends
    identifying for scenario analysis, 159
    in STEEP analysis, 176-178
turnover analysis, 75

U

uncertainties
    identifying for scenario analysis, 159
    in STEEP analysis, 174
undermining groups (issue response
    pattern), 126
universal issues, 122

V

value chain analysis
    case study, 217-219
    primary activities in, 200, 208-209
    purpose of, 199-204
    steps in, 206-216
    strengths of, 204-205
    subsets of, 203
    support activities in, 200, 210-211
    value chain links, 202
    weaknesses of, 205-206
value-creating activities, identifying
    in value chain analysis, 207
Value Line Investment Survey, 87
variables in STEEP analysis, 171
VCA. *See* value chain analysis
vertical linkage analysis in value
    chain analysis, 215-216
visual competitor strength grids, 59

W–Z

Wall Street Journal, 85
weaknesses
    defined, 191
    listing in SWOT analysis, 190-191
    ranking in SWOT analysis, 191-192
    strategy development in SWOT
        analysis, 192, 194-195
working capital, 79
Worldscope Fundamentals, 88

Xerox case study, 129

Yahoo! Finance, 85